TURNING PIPS INTO PROFIT

Forex Trading for Beginners

By
Nathan Venture, D

TURNING PIPS INTO PROFIT

Forex Trading for Beginners

CONTENTS

INTRODUCTION

Welcome to the exciting and often complex world of Forex trading. You might be here because you've heard about the potential to create significant returns or perhaps you are captivated by the idea of participating in a global market that operates 24 hours a day. Whatever your reason, this book aims to be your comprehensive guide to understanding the Forex market from the ground up.

The journey into Forex trading can be both thrilling and daunting. As a newcomer, it's likely that you have countless questions swirling around in your mind. What exactly is Forex trading? How do currency pairs work? Who are the key players? This introduction aims to clarify those initial questions and set the stage for the detailed chapters that follow.

First, let's address the fundamentals. Forex trading, short for foreign exchange trading, involves buying and selling currency pairs. The basic concept is to exchange one currency for another, hoping that the currency you bought will increase in value relative to the one you sold. This increment might seem small at first glance, but in the world of Forex, those tiny pips (percentage in points) can quickly add up to significant gains—or losses.

Understanding the structure of the Forex market is crucial for grasping how it operates. Unlike stock markets, the Forex market is decentralized. It doesn't have a central exchange. Instead, it operates through a global network of banks, brokers, and financial institutions. This decentralization offers unique advantages like around-the-clock trading and substantial liquidity but also introduces complexities that require a robust foundational knowledge.

Another essential aspect of Forex trading is recognizing the key players involved. From central banks setting interest rates to hedge funds speculating on currency movements, knowing who the major players are can provide valuable insights into market dynamics. Each player has different motivations and behaviors, which collectively influence currency prices.

To begin your trading journey, you'll need to set up a trading account and pick the right broker. This isn't a decision to be taken lightly; the right broker can make a world of difference. You'll also need to familiarize yourself with the various trading platforms and tools at your disposal. Knowledge of these fundamentals will give you the confidence to make informed decisions as you take your first steps in the Forex market.

Forex trading isn't merely about understanding currencies and market structures; it's equally about mastering the art of analysis. We will explore both fundamental and technical analysis methods. These analytical techniques provide traders with tools to predict market movements and make strategic decisions. Understanding economic indicators, geopolitical events, technical charts, and price patterns will form the backbone of your trading strategy.

Speaking of strategy, one of the most critical elements in Forex trading is developing a robust trading plan. A well-thought-out plan can dramatically improve your odds of success. Your plan should outline the types of strategies you'll employ, how you'll adapt to various market conditions, and your criteria for entering and exiting trades. Additionally, backtesting your strategy using historical data can offer invaluable insights and help refine your approach.

Trading is as much a psychological endeavor as it is a technical one. The Forex market can evoke powerful emotions like fear and greed, which can cloud judgment and lead to poor decisions. Emotional discipline, patience, and the ability to maintain focus under pressure are traits every successful trader must develop. This book delves into the psychological aspects of trading to help you cultivate a mindset geared for long-term success.

Equally important is mastering risk management techniques. Even the most promising trading strategy can lead to significant losses without proper risk management. Setting stop-loss and take-profit points, managing leverage, and adhering to the 1% risk rule are some of the techniques we'll cover. These principles will help you protect your capital and ensure that you stay in the game for the long haul.

When it comes time to execute trades, understanding the mechanics is paramount. This includes knowing the types of orders available, the best times to trade, and how to ensure optimal order execution. Mastering the mechanics will empower you to execute your trading strategy efficiently and confidently.

As you progress, you'll encounter more advanced trading concepts like using Fibonacci retracements, recognizing divergence, and understanding currency correlations. These advanced topics can offer sophisticated ways to analyze the market and fine-tune your strategies, giving you an edge that sets you apart from novice traders.

Keeping a trading journal is one of the most underrated yet powerful tools in a trader's arsenal. Recording your trades, strategies, and outcomes allows you to review your performance objectively and optimize your approaches over time. This practice can highlight strengths and weaknesses you might otherwise overlook.

Continual learning is a cornerstone of lasting success in Forex trading. The market is dynamic, influenced by countless factors ranging from economic reports to geopolitical tensions. Staying informed through financial news, online resources, forums, and webinars ensures you're always ahead of the curve, ready to adapt to new market conditions.

Of course, the road to mastering Forex trading is fraught with common pitfalls. Overtrading, failing to adapt, and neglecting risk management are mistakes even seasoned traders can fall into. By understanding these pitfalls and how to avoid them, you greatly enhance your chances of achieving long-term success.

This book aims to be more than just a textbook; it is a resource, a guide, and a mentor as you navigate the Forex world. Whether you're embarking on this journey to generate supplementary income, achieve financial independence, or explore a new skill, the knowledge and strategies contained within these pages will serve as your compass. The path may be challenging, but it's also filled with opportunities for growth, learning, and financial gain.

Your journey in Forex trading starts here. Equip yourself with the knowledge, strategies, and mindset essential for navigating the market confidently and effectively. Here's to your success and the exciting adventure that lies ahead.

CHAPTER 1:
THE WORLD OF FOREX TRADING

Welcome to the exhilarating world of Forex trading, where currencies from every corner of the globe are exchanged in a dynamic, 24-hour marketplace. If you're new to Forex, don't worry—this chapter will guide you through the foundational concepts that govern this vibrant financial landscape. Understanding how currency pairs work, the structure of the Forex market, and identifying the key players will arm you with the basic knowledge needed to start your trading journey. We're about to embark on an adventure that has the potential to be as rewarding as it is intellectually fulfilling. So, get ready to explore a market that's not only the largest but also the most liquid in the world, with daily trading volumes exceeding $6 trillion. By grasping these essential elements, you'll be well-prepared to navigate the complexities and seize the opportunities that Forex trading presents.

Understanding Currency Pairs

Understanding Currency Pairs is fundamental for anyone stepping into Forex trading. Before we delve into strategies and analysis, you need to grasp what you're dealing with: currency pairs. In Forex trading, currencies are traded in pairs, meaning you're always buying one currency and selling another. This pairing aspect might seem intimidating at first, but breaking it down can make it more manageable.

To start, let's talk about how currency pairs are quoted. Each pair comprises two parts: the base currency and the quote currency. The base currency is the first in the pair and essentially, it is the 'reference' element. For instance, in the EUR/USD pair, EUR (the

Euro) is the base currency and USD (the US Dollar) is the quote currency. When you see the price for EUR/USD as 1.2000, it means one Euro is equivalent to 1.2000 US Dollars. Basically, you need 1.2000 USD to buy one EUR.

Currencies are always quoted in pairs because you're comparing the value of one currency to another. If you're buying EUR/USD, you're buying euros and selling dollars. Conversely, when you sell EUR/USD, you're selling euros to buy dollars. This interdependency might seem like a lot to understand, but it's crucial to realize how both currencies in the pair interact to affect each other's value.

I want to mention something pivotal about the two major types of currency pairs: major and minor pairs. Major pairs involve the US Dollar paired with another primary currency, such as EUR/USD or USD/JPY (Japanese Yen). These pairs are the most traded and typically provide higher liquidity and tighter spreads, making them more attractive to beginners. Minor pairs, on the other hand, are pairs without the US Dollar. An example might include EUR/GBP (British Pound). Although these pairs see less trading activity, they can still present lucrative opportunities.

Understanding a currency pair also involves being aware of so-called "majors" and "crosses". Major pairs, as mentioned, always involve the USD, because the US Dollar is the most traded currency globally. Cross currency pairs (crosses), meanwhile, exclude the USD. An example includes EUR/JPY, where you're trading the Euro against the Japanese Yen. Crosses are particularly useful when you're looking to trade that involve non-USD pairs, thereby offering diverse opportunities to profit from global market movements.

An important concept to grasp when trading currency pairs is the bid-ask spread. The bid price is the highest price that a buyer is willing to pay for a currency pair, and the ask price is the lowest price a seller is willing to accept. The difference between these two prices is known as the spread. In practical terms, the spread represents the cost of trading. A tighter spread means lower cost and better liquidity, which is favorable, especially for new traders.

By now, you might be wondering about how currency pairs are classified beyond just major and minor. That's where exotic pairs come into the picture. Exotic pairs include a major currency paired with the currency of a developing or smaller economy, like USD/TRY (Turkish Lira) or USD/ZAR (South African Rand). These pairs can offer high volatility and the potential for significant profits but can also be more unpredictable and less liquid than majors and minors.

The understanding of currency pairs extends beyond knowing what each pair represents to how they behave under different market conditions. Some pairs are more volatile than others because of the economic stability of the countries involved or geopolitical events affecting them. For example, pairs involving emerging market currencies can see greater price swings, offering opportunities for higher gains but also increased risk.

With each currency pair, it's essential to understand the factors that can cause their values to fluctuate. Economic indicators such as GDP growth, unemployment rates, interest rates, and consumer sentiment can impact the currency values. Political stability, changes in government, and geopolitical tensions also play pivotal roles. For instance, an unexpected political event in the Eurozone might create a ripple effect across EUR currency pairs.

Keep in mind that each currency in a pair has its own unique characteristics. For instance, the Japanese Yen is often seen as a safe-haven currency, meaning it tends to strengthen during times of market uncertainty. The Australian Dollar, conversely, is often more tied to commodities markets because of Australia's export-driven economy. As a beginner, recognizing these individual traits can vastly improve your market analysis and decision-making process.

Another key aspect to consider is market trading sessions. The Forex market operates 24 hours a day, five days a week, with major trading sessions in Sydney, Tokyo, London, and New York.

Currency pairs can behave differently depending on the active session. For example, during the London session, there could be higher volatility in pairs like GBP/USD or EUR/USD given the economic activities occurring in these regions.

To sum up, understanding currency pairs forms the bedrock of Forex trading. It might feel overwhelming to juggle between various terms and factors at first, but take your time with each concept. Achieving a solid understanding here will set a strong foundation for delving deeper into the Forex market, enabling you to feel more confident. This knowledge will pave the way for you to tackle more advanced concepts like technical and fundamental analysis in future chapters effectively.

The Structure of the Forex Market

The Structure of the Forex Market is pivotal to understand before diving into the intricacies of trading. Unlike stock markets, which are centralized, the Forex market operates on a decentralized network of banks, financial institutions, brokers, and individual traders. This unique structure leads to a dynamic and fluid market environment that spans the globe, operating 24 hours a day, five days a week.

At its core, the Forex market consists of the interbank market and the over-the-counter (OTC) market. The interbank market involves large financial institutions trading currencies directly with each other. This segment of the market is responsible for a substantial volume of daily Forex transactions. On the other hand, the OTC market, which includes retail traders like you, operates through a network of brokers and dealers who facilitate currency trades outside of centralized exchanges.

Understanding the layers within the Forex market helps grasp the roles of different participants. The top-tier consists of central banks and major financial institutions. Central banks, such as the Federal Reserve, the European Central Bank, and the Bank of Japan, influence Forex through monetary policy, interest rates, and currency interventions. Their actions can cause significant market

BOLLINGER BANDS

LENGTH 200

STD DEV 2

shifts, making it essential for traders to stay informed about central bank activities.

Next in line are the commercial banks and investment banks. These entities execute trades on behalf of their clients and engage in proprietary trading, seeking profits from currency fluctuations. Many of the market-making activities, where they quote both buy and sell prices, occur at this level. Market makers play a critical role in ensuring liquidity, allowing trades to be executed swiftly even in volatile market conditions.

Below the banks are the hedge funds, corporations, and institutional investors. Hedge funds are known for their aggressive trading strategies and significant market influence, often moving large amounts of money rapidly. Corporations participate in the Forex market primarily for hedging purposes, protecting themselves against unfavorable currency movements that could affect their international business operations. Institutional investors, like pension funds and endowment funds, engage in Forex for portfolio diversification and risk management.

Lastly, we come to retail traders, the individuals who buy and sell currencies through online platforms. Retail Forex brokers provide access to the Forex market and offer various trading tools and educational resources. While retail traders account for a smaller portion of the market volume, their collective impact and the democratization of trading have grown significantly over recent years.

The decentralized nature of Forex trading implies that there isn't a single exchange where all transactions occur. Instead, transactions are processed via electronic trading systems, also known as electronic communication networks (ECNs), and through direct trading with brokers. This structure enables continuous operation across various time zones, from the Asian markets opening on Sunday evening until the U.S. markets close on Friday night.

The market is divided into four primary trading sessions: the Sydney session, the Tokyo session, the London session, and the

9

New York session. Each session has its own characteristics and trading dynamics. For instance, the overlap between the London and New York sessions tends to be the most active and liquid period, offering numerous trading opportunities due to high market participation and significant news releases.

While the Forex market offers unparalleled access and trading hours, it's essential to understand the implications of trading in a decentralized environment. Liquidity, volatility, and price spreads can vary significantly based on the time of day and activity levels in different market centers. Smart traders learn to identify the optimal times to trade specific currency pairs, maximizing their chances of success.

Furthermore, technological advancements have played a crucial role in shaping the Forex market's structure. Automated trading systems, algorithmic trading, and high-frequency trading (HFT) have become integral components. These technologies enhance market efficiency but also introduce complexities and competition. Understanding how these systems work can give traders an edge in navigating the modern Forex landscape.

In conclusion, grasping **The Structure of the Forex Market** provides a solid foundation for anyone stepping into currency trading. Recognizing the various participants and their roles, along with the decentralized nature of the market, contributes to informed decision-making. As you continue your journey into Forex, keep this structure in mind, and remember that knowledge and awareness are your allies in navigating the vibrant and ever-changing world of currency trading.

Major Players in Forex

The Forex market is a vast, globally interconnected environment where myriad entities participate, each with its unique motivations and objectives. Understanding who these major players are is crucial for anyone stepping into the world of currency trading. These participants can broadly be categorized into governments and central banks, commercial banks, hedge funds, corporations, and retail traders. Each of these players plays a significant role in shaping market movements and liquidity.

Governments and central banks are among the most influential participants in the Forex market. Central banks, such as the Federal Reserve in the United States, the European Central Bank, and the Bank of Japan, control the monetary policy of their respective countries. They manage currency reserves and set interest rates, which have direct impacts on currency values. When central banks intervene in the market by buying or selling their currency, it can cause significant fluctuations. For instance, a decision to lower interest rates can lead to a depreciation of the national currency as it becomes less attractive to investors.

Commercial banks are another critical component. Banks such as HSBC, JPMorgan Chase, and BNP Paribas engage in Forex trading both to facilitate business transactions and to speculate for profit. They provide liquidity to the market by buying and selling currencies on behalf of their clients, including corporations, hedge funds, and individual traders. These banks operate in the interbank market, the highest tier of the Forex market, where large volumes of currency are traded, often in multi-million-dollar transactions. Because of their sheer volume and capital, their actions can sway market trends and create shifts in currency values.

Hedge funds are private investment funds that use sophisticated strategies to maximize returns for their clients. These funds often engage in speculative trading, leveraging large sums of money to capitalize on currency movements. Entities like Bridgewater Associates and Soros Fund Management have been known to influence the Forex market significantly. As they make massive trades based on their market predictions, they can drive significant trends and volatility, affecting other participants in the process. Their strategies can include anything from leveraging interest rate differentials to capitalizing on geopolitical events.

Corporations participate in Forex primarily for operational purposes rather than speculation. Multinational companies like Apple, Toyota, and Unilever need to engage in currency trading to manage the risks associated with their global operations. They might need to convert revenues generated in foreign currencies back to their home currency or hedge against potential fluctuations to protect their profit margins. While corporations usually make smaller trades compared to banks and hedge funds, the overall volume of corporate transactions still makes a significant impact on the market.

Finally, we arrive at retail traders, a group that includes people like you. Thanks to technological advancements and the proliferation of online trading platforms, individuals now have easy access to the Forex market. While retail traders typically trade in smaller amounts compared to institutional participants, their collective activity can contribute significantly to market liquidity. Retail brokers facilitate these transactions, providing the necessary tools and platforms for individual traders to engage in Forex trading.

The role of retail traders has grown considerably over the years, spurred by greater access to information and trading education. Despite being relatively small players in the grand scheme of things, retail traders have the advantage of flexibility. They can quickly adapt to market changes and employ various trading strategies, ranging from day trading to long-term investing. However, retail traders need to be well-informed, disciplined, and strategic to succeed in this fast-paced market.

Collaboration and conflict among these major players create the dynamic and ever-changing environment that characterizes the Forex market. For instance, a central bank's decision to adjust interest rates might be scrutinized by hedge funds looking for arbitrage opportunities or counter-moves. Similarly, a multinational corporation hedging its currency exposure can trigger movements that affect both retail traders and large financial institutions. This interconnectedness emphasizes the importance of staying informed and understanding the underlying factors influencing currency movements.

One cannot overlook the role of electronic trading systems and automated trading algorithms in shaping the current Forex landscape. Banks, hedge funds, and even some sophisticated retail traders employ algorithms to execute trade strategies based on predefined criteria. These algorithms can process vast amounts of data in real-time, identify trading opportunities, and execute transactions faster than any human could. While algorithmic trading brings efficiency and liquidity to the market, it also introduces risks such as sudden market swings driven by automated responses to economic data or geopolitical events.

Regulatory bodies also play a pivotal role, although they're not market participants per se. Organizations like the Commodity Futures Trading Commission (CFTC) in the United States or the Financial Conduct Authority (FCA) in the UK provide oversight to ensure market integrity and protect traders from fraud. Their influence helps maintain a level of fairness and transparency, making the Forex market a more secure environment for all participants.

In summary, the Forex market's complexity and size are shaped by the diverse objectives and strategies of its major players—governments and central banks, commercial banks, hedge funds, corporations, and retail traders. By understanding who these players are and what motivates them, you can gain valuable insights into market movements and develop more effective trading strategies. The key to success lies in recognizing these dynamics and staying adaptable to the ever-evolving landscape of Forex trading.

CHAPTER 2:
GETTING STARTED IN FOREX

Venturing into the Forex market starts with some essential groundwork. First and foremost, you'll need to set up your trading account—this acts as your gateway to the world of currency trading. Picking the right Forex broker is crucial since they differ in terms of services, fees, and trading conditions. Take the time to research and choose one that aligns with your trading goals. Equally important are the trading platforms and tools you'll be using. These platforms are more than just interfaces; they're the instruments through which you execute your trades and analyze the market. Getting familiar with these tools early on will streamline your trading process and enhance your decision-making capabilities. By setting a solid foundation, you'll be better equipped to navigate the complexities of the Forex market with confidence and clarity.

Setting Up Your Trading Account

Setting Up Your Trading Account is the crucial first step in your journey into forex trading. To begin, you'll need a trading account with a reputable broker that complements your individual needs and preferences. Establishing this account is akin to preparing your toolkit before embarking on a new endeavor. Each piece of information you provide and each step you take now will lay the foundation for your trading experience.

First, decide on the type of account you need. Brokers often offer different account types—standard, mini, or micro accounts—depending on your bankroll and risk tolerance. Standard accounts might demand higher minimum deposits but come with perks like advanced trading tools and tighter spreads. Micro accounts, meanwhile, allow for smaller trades and are ideal for beginners to get a feel of the market without exposing themselves to large financial risks.

Next, you'll need to provide some paperwork to get things going. Typically, brokers require identification documents, such as a valid passport or driver's license, and proof of address, like a utility bill or bank statement. Verification is a critical step for ensuring the security and legality of your trading activities. This process helps prevent fraud and ensures compliance with regulatory frameworks.

Once you've submitted all the necessary documents, you'll proceed to fund your account. Funding methods vary across brokers, but common options include bank transfers, credit/debit cards, and e-wallets like PayPal. Select a funding option that offers low fees and quick processing times. Additionally, familiarize yourself with the broker's withdrawal process as you'll want to know how to access your funds whenever needed.

Many brokers offer demo accounts, which allow you to trade with virtual money. Take advantage of these demo accounts to familiarize yourself with the trading platform and test your strategies without the risk of losing real money. This step is invaluable for beginners as it provides a risk-free environment to learn the ropes of forex trading.

Now, consider the trading platform you will use. Brokers typically provide platforms like MetaTrader 4 (MT4), MetaTrader 5 (MT5), or proprietary platforms. Each comes with unique features and interfaces. MT4 and MT5 are popular for their robust analytical tools and user-friendly layout, making them excellent choices for beginners and experienced traders alike. Proprietary platforms might offer unique features that could suit your specific trading style.

Additionally, ensure that your broker offers a mobile trading platform. In today's fast-paced world, having the flexibility to manage your trades from your smartphone is invaluable. Mobile platforms allow you to monitor the market and execute trades on the go, ensuring you don't miss out on potential opportunities.

Security cannot be emphasized enough when setting up your trading account. Enable two-factor authentication (2FA) if your trading platform offers it. This adds an extra layer of security, protecting your account from unauthorized access. Keeping your software and devices updated is equally important. Security updates often fix vulnerabilities that can be exploited by malicious entities.

After you've established your account and are comfortable with the demo trading environment, you'll need to dive into the real trading world. Start small. Begin by trading micro-lots to get accustomed to the emotional and psychological aspects of trading in a real market. It's easy to get excited and want to dive in headfirst, but keeping your initial trades small and manageable can help you learn without taking on too much risk.

You're now ready to set up your trading environment. Create a dedicated space where you can focus on your trades without distraction. A dual-monitor setup can be beneficial, allowing you to keep multiple data streams and charts open concurrently. High-speed internet is a must to ensure that you can execute trades promptly without lag.

Finally, make sure you have access to reliable customer support from your broker. Issues can arise at any time, and having a dedicated support team available can be a lifesaver. Test their responsiveness through some inquiries before committing to their services. Knowing you can rely on them provides peace of mind as you navigate the complexities of forex trading.

In summary, setting up your trading account correctly is a blend of strategic decisions and practical setup steps. From choosing the right account type to ensuring robust security measures, each step plays a pivotal role in your trading journey. By taking the time to set up your account properly, you're laying a solid foundation for effective and confident forex trading. Your journey has just begun, and with the right preparations, you're poised to tackle the forex market with steadfastness and informed insight.

Choosing the Right Forex Broker

Choosing the Right Forex Broker is a crucial step in building your foundation in Forex trading. Before diving into the currency markets, it's essential to select a broker that meets your needs and preferences. A broker serves as your gateway to the Forex market, offering the platform and tools you need to execute trades, manage your portfolio, and access valuable market information. Without the right broker, even the best trading strategies can falter. Here, we'll dissect the key factors to consider when making your choice, setting you up for a smoother trading experience.

Your first consideration should be the broker's regulatory status. In the Forex world, regulation is a sign of credibility and trustworthiness. Regulatory bodies, such as the National Futures Association (NFA) and the Commodity Futures Trading Commission (CFTC) in the United States, or the Financial Conduct Authority (FCA) in the UK, ensure that brokers adhere to strict standards, protecting your funds and personal information. Confirming your broker is regulated by a recognized authority can save you from potential scams and fraudulent activities.

Next on the checklist is the broker's trading platform. The trading platform is your primary interface with the Forex market, so it should be user-friendly, intuitive, and packed with the features you need. MetaTrader 4 and MetaTrader 5 are popular choices among traders for their comprehensive charting tools and automated trading capabilities. Some brokers also offer proprietary platforms that could cater to specific trading needs. It's wise to test out a few platforms through demo accounts before committing to one—this hands-on experience can highlight strengths and weaknesses that aren't evident on paper.

Another crucial factor is trading costs. Brokers typically earn money through spreads and commissions. The spread is the difference between the bid and ask prices of a currency pair, while commissions are a flat fee per trade. Some brokers offer tight spreads but charge higher commissions, while others offer commission-free trading with higher spreads. Beginners should weigh these costs in relation to their trading frequency and style to ensure profitability isn't eroded by excessive fees. Also, don't forget to check for hidden fees such as withdrawal fees or inactivity charges.

Liquidity is another key consideration, particularly if you plan to trade higher volumes or want to ensure faster execution speeds. High liquidity usually translates to better pricing and less slippage, which occurs when trades are executed at different prices than expected. Brokers with strong connections to liquidity providers are generally more reliable in terms of execution quality. This can make a significant difference, especially during volatile market conditions when prices can change rapidly.

The range of available trading instruments is also important. While you're primarily focusing on Forex, having access to other financial instruments like commodities, indices, or cryptocurrencies can diversify your portfolio and provide additional trading opportunities. A broker offering a wide variety of assets allows you to exploit different market conditions and hedge your positions effectively.

Consider the broker's customer service and support. As a beginner, you may have numerous questions and encounter issues requiring immediate assistance. A broker with responsive and knowledgeable customer support can make your trading journey far less stressful. Look for brokers offering 24/7 support through various channels such as live chat, email, and phone. Forums and online reviews can also provide candid insights into the quality of a broker's customer service.

Education and research tools provided by the broker can be invaluable. Many reputable brokers offer educational content, including webinars, articles, and tutorials aimed at helping traders improve their skills. Additionally, access to market analysis, real-time news feeds, and economic calendars can enhance your trading strategy and decision-making process. Brokers invested in the success of their clients often provide these resources, fostering a more informed trading environment.

Leverage options offered by brokers can significantly impact your trading strategy. While leverage allows you to control a large position with a relatively small amount of capital, it also magnifies your risk. Beginners should be cautious with high leverage levels, ensuring the broker's leverage options are flexible and align with their risk tolerance. New traders might prefer brokers offering lower leverage options to mitigate risks while they learn.

Security of funds is another critical factor. Reputable brokers often segregate client funds from their operating capital, adding an extra layer of protection in the event of financial instability or insolvency. Look for brokers who have transparent policies regarding fund protection and clearly state their practices on their websites or in their customer agreements.

Finally, it's essential to verify the ease of deposits and withdrawals. A broker that complicates the process of moving your money is a red flag. Evaluate the variety of payment methods supported, including credit/debit cards, bank transfers, and e-wallets and observe any associated processing times or fees. Efficient deposit and withdrawal processes ensure that funds are accessible when you need them, providing peace of mind as you navigate the Forex market.

Choosing the right Forex broker is not a decision to be taken lightly. It involves careful consideration of various factors that collectively influence your trading experience and potential success. By thoroughly researching and evaluating brokers based on their regulatory status, platform features, trading costs, liquidity, range of instruments, customer support, educational resources, leverage options, fund security, and transaction processes, you can make a more informed choice.

Ultimately, the goal is to find a broker that aligns with your trading style and goals, providing a secure, efficient, and supportive environment. Remember, the right broker can enhance your trading experience, offering the tools and support necessary to thrive in the dynamic world of Forex trading. Take your time and choose wisely—this foundational step will pave the way for your future success in the Forex market.

Key Trading Platforms and Tools

Key Trading Platforms and Tools in Forex trading, having the right tools at your disposal is crucial. The right trading platform can mean the difference between a seamless trading experience and one filled with frustration and missed opportunities. With countless trading platforms available, choosing the one that best suits your needs can be daunting. However, by understanding the key features and tools that top platforms offer, you can make an informed decision.

One of the most popular and widely used trading platforms is MetaTrader 4 (MT4). MT4 is favored by both beginners and experienced traders due to its user-friendly interface and robust set of features. The platform offers multiple charting tools, indicators, and automated trading capabilities via Expert Advisors (EAs). Its popularity ensures a wealth of online resources and community support, making it an excellent choice for those new to Forex.

MetaTrader 5 (MT5) is often seen as the successor to MT4, offering additional features and improvements. While retaining the core functionalities of MT4, MT5 includes more timeframes, advanced order types, and a more extensive economic calendar. It also supports trading in other markets beyond Forex, such as stocks and commodities, giving you more flexibility if you decide to diversify your trading portfolio down the line.

For traders who prefer web-based platforms, TradingView is an excellent option. TradingView stands out due to its highly interactive and visually appealing charts. It offers a wide range of technical analysis tools and the ability to create custom indicators using the Pine Script programming language. Moreover, its social networking features allow traders to share ideas and strategies, fostering a community of collaborative learning.

If you're looking for a platform that excels in speed and reliability, consider cTrader. Known for its transparent pricing model and advanced charting tools, cTrader also boasts features like Level II pricing and algorithmic trading support through its cAlgo platform. This makes it particularly appealing for traders who rely on high-frequency and algorithmic trading strategies.

Apart from these well-known platforms, many brokers provide proprietary trading platforms designed to meet the specific needs of their clients. These custom platforms often come with unique tools and features that can give you an edge. For example, some may offer specialized news feeds, in-house analysis, and exclusive indicators not available on other platforms. It's always worth exploring the options provided by your broker to see if their proprietary tools align with your trading style.

Now, let's talk about essential tools that can enhance your trading experience. One indispensable tool is a reliable economic calendar. Economic calendars list upcoming economic events and data releases that can impact currency prices. By staying informed about these events, you can better anticipate market movements and adjust your trading strategy accordingly. Many platforms, including MT4, MT5, and TradingView, offer built-in economic calendars, ensuring you have this critical information at your fingertips.

Another crucial tool is backtesting software. Backtesting allows you to test your trading strategies against historical data to see how they would have performed in the past. This can provide valuable insights and help you refine your strategy before risking real capital. Platforms like MT4 and MT5 include built-in backtesting capabilities, or you can use specialized backtesting software for more advanced analysis.

Risk management tools are also vital for successful trading. One common risk management tool is the stop-loss order, which automatically closes a trade when it reaches a predefined loss level. This helps limit your losses and protect your capital. Similarly, a take-profit order automatically closes a trade when it reaches a predefined profit level, ensuring you lock in gains. Many platforms allow you to set these orders easily, making risk management an integral part of your trading routine.

Automation tools can significantly enhance your trading efficiency. Expert Advisors (EAs) in MT4 and MT5 allow you to automate trading strategies, removing emotion from decision-making and ensuring consistency. You can either create your own EAs using the MQL4/MQL5 programming languages or purchase them from marketplaces. Similarly, algorithmic trading tools available on platforms like cTrader enable you to implement and execute complex trading algorithms with precision.

For those who seek to integrate news and data analytics into their trading, platforms that offer built-in news feeds and analytics tools are invaluable. Access to real-time news updates from reliable sources can help you stay ahead of market-moving events. Platforms like MT5 and TradingView offer integrated news feeds, while others might provide access to premium news services for a fee.

Charting tools are the backbone of technical analysis, and having access to advanced charting capabilities can greatly improve your trading decisions. Look for platforms that offer customizable charts, a wide range of technical indicators, and the ability to draw trend lines and patterns. The ability to save and retrieve chart templates is also useful for quickly applying your preferred analysis setup.

Lastly, educational tools and resources can be a game-changer, especially for beginners. Many platforms and brokers offer a wealth of educational materials, including tutorials, webinars, and demo accounts. These resources can help you get up to speed on platform features, trading strategies, and market analysis techniques. Taking advantage of these educational tools can accelerate your learning and boost your confidence as you navigate the Forex market.

In conclusion, selecting the right trading platform and tools tailored to your needs can make a significant impact on your Forex trading journey. Whether you prioritize user-friendly interfaces, advanced charting capabilities, or automation features, there's a platform out there that suits your trading style. Don't hesitate to explore and test different platforms through demo accounts to find the best fit for you. Your trading success is built on a solid foundation of the right tools, continuous learning, and consistent practice.

CHAPTER 3:
FUNDAMENTAL ANALYSIS

Venturing into the realm of fundamental analysis, we uncover the essential tools and insights that allow traders to interpret and anticipate market movements based on underlying economic realities. This type of analysis hinges on understanding economic indicators, political and geopolitical events, and the policies and decisions of central banks, all of which can cause significant fluctuations in currency values. By mastering the evaluation of such factors, beginners can start to see the Forex market not just as a series of numbers and charts, but as a complex, interconnected system influenced by real-world developments. It's about developing a deeper intuition for why currencies behave the way they do, empowering traders to make more informed, strategic decisions. So, as we delve into the mechanisms of fundamental analysis, remember that every economic report, political event, and central bank decision tells a part of the Forex story that can help you navigate the markets with greater confidence and acumen.

Economic Indicators and Their Impact

Economic Indicators and Their Impact are vital components in the toolkit of any successful forex trader. These indicators, released by governments and private institutions, offer insights into a country's economic health, influence currency values, and affect market sentiment. Understanding these indicators allows traders to forecast currency movements and make informed trading decisions.

Economic indicators come in various forms, each gauging different aspects of economic performance. For example, gross domestic product (GDP) measures the overall economic output of a country. A rising GDP typically signals economic strength, boosting a nation's currency. Conversely, a declining GDP may indicate economic struggles, potentially weakening the currency. But it's not just about the absolute numbers—the rate of change and market expectations also play significant roles.

Inflation indicators, such as the Consumer Price Index (CPI) and the Producer Price Index (PPI), provide crucial data on price stability and purchasing power. Inflation that is too high can erode currency value as it diminishes real returns on investments. On the other hand, stable, low inflation is usually favorable for a currency. Central banks often respond to inflation trends by adjusting interest rates, further influencing forex markets.

Employment statistics also serve as key economic indicators, with non-farm payroll (NFP) data from the United States being particularly influential. High employment rates generally signal economic stability and growth, strengthening the currency. On release days, the NFP report can cause significant market volatility. A savvy trader needs to monitor these events closely and plan their trades accordingly.

Interest rates themselves are powerful indicators. Central banks, such as the Federal Reserve in the United States or the European Central Bank, set benchmark interest rates to control monetary policy. Higher interest rates tend to attract foreign investment, increasing demand for the domestic currency, while lower rates may deter investment and weaken the currency. Traders should keep a keen eye on central bank announcements and minutes from meetings, as these often provide hints about future monetary policy changes.

Trade balances, which measure the difference between a country's exports and imports, also affect currency values. A trade surplus—where exports exceed imports—generally strengthens a nation's currency as it indicates greater demand for goods and services. A trade deficit, however, can weaken a currency, as it signifies higher demand for foreign products. Monitoring these balances helps traders anticipate currency movements and adjust their strategies.

Consumer confidence indices reflect the optimism or pessimism of consumers regarding their economic prospects. High consumer confidence suggests economic growth, as consumers are more likely to spend, stimulating the economy and potentially strengthening the currency. Conversely, low confidence can signal economic trouble and a weaker currency. This indicator can be particularly useful for traders to gauge future economic trends.

Another important aspect to consider is the impact of geopolitical events. While these are not traditional economic indicators, political instability, international conflicts, or changes in government policies can have profound effects on a country's economy and, consequently, its currency. Staying informed about global political events is crucial for anticipating sudden market shifts.

It's also essential to distinguish between leading and lagging indicators. Leading indicators, such as manufacturing activity indexes like the Purchasing Managers' Index (PMI), provide early signals of economic trends. They help forex traders anticipate future market conditions. Lagging indicators, like GDP, provide confirmation of economic patterns but might lag behind current market conditions. Balancing data from both types of indicators can lead to more accurate forecasts.

While understanding economic indicators is crucial, it's also important to pair this knowledge with other analytical tools. Fundamental analysis using these indicators should be complemented by technical analysis, which examines price charts and patterns. This dual approach can enhance trade accuracy and profitability.

Economic indicators don't operate in isolation. Their impact on currency markets is interconnected, and one indicator can influence another. For instance, high employment rates might lead to increased consumer spending, boosting GDP. Similarly, inflation might prompt central banks to adjust interest rates, impacting currency values. Keeping a holistic view helps traders understand the broader economic landscape.

Frequent releases of economic data create opportunities for astute traders. Scheduled economic reports can lead to increased market volatility, offering potential trading setups. Speculating on the outcome of these reports can be risky, but well-informed traders can use this volatility to their advantage, making trades based on expected market reactions.

It's prudent for traders to maintain an economic calendar, which lists the dates and times of key indicator releases. This helps them prepare for potential market movements. Online platforms usually offer customizable economic calendars, allowing traders to focus on the most relevant indicators for their trading strategy.

While economic indicators provide valuable insights, they are not infallible. Unexpected events or market sentiments can cause actual market outcomes to deviate from predicted ones. Therefore, it's important to use indicators as part of a broader trading strategy that includes risk management and continuous learning.

In summary, **Economic Indicators and Their Impact** on forex trading cannot be overstated. They offer essential data points that help traders forecast market movements and make informed decisions. By understanding and interpreting these indicators, combining them with technical analysis, and staying informed about geopolitical events, new traders can navigate the forex market with confidence and acumen. The journey may seem complex, but with diligence and the right knowledge, it is entirely manageable.

Political and Geopolitical Events

Political and Geopolitical Events are a potent force in the world of Forex trading. When you start trading currencies, you'll quickly realize that the value of money is not just influenced by economic factors but also by what happens politically and geopolitically around the globe. Currency values can swing dramatically due to elections, policy changes, international conflicts, treaties, and even rumors of such events.

Take elections, for instance. The outcome of an election can shift the economic policies of a country, which, in turn, influences currency values. In the lead-up to an election, you might see increased volatility in a country's currency as traders try to predict the outcomes and adjust their positions accordingly. Once the results are in, if the elected party is expected to pursue economic policies that favor growth, such as tax cuts or increased government spending, the currency might see a bullish trend. Conversely, if the policies are expected to hurt economic growth, the currency might depreciate.

Let's not forget international relations. Diplomatic tensions, trade negotiations, sanctions, or military conflicts can all have immediate and long-lasting impacts on currency values. For example, when two countries engage in a trade war, currencies can become extremely volatile. Tariffs and trade barriers generally lead to economic uncertainty, which traders detest, resulting in a more tumultuous market. Therefore, keeping an eye on international news is essential for making informed trades.

Another significant factor is government stability and integrity. Countries experiencing political turmoil often see their currencies fall. Situations like a coup d'état, prolonged protests, or even corruption scandals can sow doubt among investors and traders, leading to a rapid outflow of capital. Stability fosters confidence, and confidence drives investment, both domestically and internationally. So, if a country is seen as stable and well-governed, its currency is likely to be stronger.

Policy changes, especially those concerning fiscal and monetary issues, are critical too. When a government announces new policies related to taxes, spending, or regulation, the markets take notice. For instance, policies that are seen to support economic growth can be favorable for the currency. On the other hand, policies that create economic restrictions or unpredictability can lead to a rapid depreciation of the currency.

Geopolitical events also come into play in the Forex market. Consider the influence of large international organizations and agreements like the European Union, NAFTA, or the Trans-Pacific Partnership. When countries join or leave these organizations, or when new agreements are signed, the currencies of the involved nations can experience significant shifts. Brexit, for example, led to substantial volatility in the British Pound as traders tried to gauge the economic impact of the UK leaving the EU.

Trading sanctions are another powerful tool in the geopolitical arsenal, often leaving a considerable mark on currency values. For example, a country heavily reliant on exports might see its currency weaken if sanctions constrain its trading ability. In contrast, a nation imposing the sanctions might experience an initial economic hit but could ultimately benefit if it positions itself as a more stable or more ethical trading partner.

It's also vital to understand the broader impacts of military actions. While the immediate effect of conflict is usually negative leading to a flight-to-safety, where traders flock to currencies considered safe havens like the US Dollar, Yen, or Swiss Franc, the longer-term impacts can be varied. Nations engaged in prolonged conflict often face economic difficulties, leading to weaker currencies. Conversely, countries seen as neutral or uninvolved might benefit as their currencies strengthen relative to those embroiled in conflict.

It's not enough to only react to these events; anticipation and preparation are key. Successful traders often speculate on political and geopolitical developments, positioning themselves ahead of major announcements or anticipated events. This proactive approach requires staying informed through reliable news sources and fostering a keen understanding of global political trends.

Moreover, it's important not to overlook the role of political rhetoric and promises. Political leaders and candidates sometimes make statements or promises that can sway market sentiment even before any tangible actions are taken. For instance, promises of deregulation, monetary stimulus, or fiscal austerity can significantly impact currency values based on market perceptions of how these policies will influence economic stability and growth.

Don't underestimate the impact of globalization and interconnected markets. A political or geopolitical event in one country can have cascading effects on other currencies. For instance, a financial crisis in a major economy like the US or China can lead to global market instability, influencing currencies worldwide. Similarly, regional conflicts can have broader implications, affecting international trade routes and global supply chains, which in turn impact currency values.

For beginners in Forex trading, understanding the political and geopolitical landscape can seem daunting. However, incorporating these elements into your trading strategy can offer a significant edge. The key is to remain vigilant and reactive without being overly speculative. Use a combination of reliable news sources and robust analytical tools to stay ahead of political developments. Formulate strategies that account for possible outcomes, and always be ready to adapt as situations evolve.

In summary, political and geopolitical events are influential forces in the Forex market. They can create both opportunities and risks. Successful traders are those who can anticipate these movements, interpret their implications correctly, and react swiftly and effectively. By integrating political and geopolitical analysis into your trading strategy, you enhance your ability to navigate the complexities of the Forex market with confidence and skill.

Central Banks and Interest Rates

Central Banks and Interest Rates play a crucial role in the Forex market, and understanding their dynamics is key to making informed trading decisions. Central banks, such as the Federal Reserve in the United States, the European Central Bank, and the Bank of Japan, oversee monetary policy in their respective countries. Their primary tools include setting interest rates, controlling money supply, and influencing inflation rates. These decisions can significantly impact currency values and, consequently, the Forex market.

Interest rates are perhaps the most closely watched economic indicator by Forex traders. When a central bank adjusts its interest rates, it sends ripples across global financial markets. Higher interest rates generally attract foreign investment, increasing demand for that country's currency and pushing its value higher. Conversely, lower interest rates tend to discourage foreign investment, leading to a decrease in currency value. For example, if the Federal Reserve raises interest rates, the U.S. dollar may appreciate as investors seek higher returns on investments denominated in dollars.

Central banks use interest rates to control inflation and stabilize their countries' economies. Inflation is the rate at which the general level of prices for goods and services rises, leading to a decrease in purchasing power. If inflation rises too quickly, central banks may raise interest rates to cool down the economy. Higher borrowing costs reduce consumer and business spending, which can help tame inflation. On the other hand, if inflation is too low or if the economy is in a recession, central banks may lower interest rates to encourage borrowing and spending, hoping to spur economic growth.

It's important to note that central bank decisions are not made in a vacuum. These institutions analyze a vast array of economic data, including employment figures, GDP growth, retail sales, and other key indicators, to gauge the health of the economy. Traders closely follow these data releases because they can provide clues about future central bank actions. For instance, a strong jobs report might lead to speculation that a rate hike is on the horizon, while weak economic data could suggest a rate cut.

Another critical aspect of central bank influence in Forex is forward guidance. This refers to the communication strategy used by central banks to signal their future monetary policy intentions. By issuing statements, press releases, or holding press conferences, central banks provide the market with insights into their economic outlook and policy direction. Traders use this forward guidance to adjust their trading strategies. For instance, if the European Central Bank hints at future rate hikes, traders might start buying Euros in anticipation of higher returns.

Central banks' decisions can also have a psychological impact on the market. Even the anticipation of an interest rate change can cause significant market fluctuations. Forex markets are driven by expectations, and traders often "price in" expected rate changes well before they happen. This means that the actual interest rate decision might have a different impact than initially anticipated, depending on whether it aligns with or deviates from market expectations.

A notable example of central bank influence is the "carry trade" strategy. This involves borrowing money in a currency with low-interest rates and investing it in a currency with higher interest rates. The goal is to profit from the interest rate differential. While central banks may not directly encourage carry trades, their interest rate policies create the conditions that make such strategies viable. However, carry trades can be risky; if the central bank of the high-interest-rate currency decides to cut rates unexpectedly, the value of that currency could plummet.

Market intervention is another tool central banks occasionally use to influence the value of their currency. This can involve buying or selling large quantities of their own currency in the foreign exchange market. For example, the Swiss National Bank has intervened in the past to prevent the Swiss Franc from becoming too strong, which could harm their export-driven economy. While such interventions can be effective in the short term, they often signal deeper economic issues that traders need to be aware of.

It's also worth mentioning the concept of "quantitative easing" (QE), where central banks purchase longer-term securities from the open market to increase the money supply and encourage lending and investment. QE can have a similar effect to lowering interest rates and is typically used when traditional monetary policy tools have been exhausted. For example, during the 2008 financial crisis, many central banks employed QE to support their economies, which had a notable impact on exchange rates and the Forex market.

In summary, understanding how central banks and interest rates influence the Forex market is essential for any trader. These institutions' decisions can drive significant currency movements, present trading opportunities, and carry risks. Traders need to stay informed about central bank announcements, economic indicators, and global economic conditions to make educated trading decisions. By closely monitoring these factors, you can better anticipate market trends and react effectively to changes in monetary policy.

CHAPTER 4:
TECHNICAL ANALYSIS BASICS

Technical analysis is the cornerstone of many traders' strategies, offering a structured approach to understanding market movements through historical price data and chart patterns. In this chapter, you'll learn the essentials of reading forex charts, identifying support and resistance levels, and recognizing trend lines and price patterns. These skills are crucial for predicting future market behaviors and making informed trading decisions. By grasping the foundations of technical analysis, you'll equip yourself with powerful tools to detect market trends, optimize entry and exit points, and ultimately enhance your trading performance. This isn't just about numbers and lines; it's about gaining an edge in a competitive market, transforming analytical insights into lucrative trading opportunities.

Reading Forex Charts

Reading Forex Charts is an essential skill for any new trader. Understanding how to read and interpret these charts is like learning the language of the Forex market—it's foundational to making informed trading decisions. Forex charts provide a visual representation of currency price movements over time, and they can vary in complexity from simple line charts to intricate candlestick charts.

The first step in reading Forex charts is familiarizing yourself with the different types. The most commonly used chart types are line charts, bar charts, and candlestick charts. Each has its advantages and nuances, making them suitable for different trading styles and strategies. For beginners, starting with line charts can be beneficial as they offer a straightforward representation of price movements. Line charts plot a single line by connecting closing prices over a specified period, providing an uncluttered view of the overall trend. However, they lack detailed information that other charts offer.

Bar charts introduce more complexity by showing not just the closing price, but also the opening price, and the highs and lows of a specified time period. Each bar represents one period (e.g., one hour) and consists of a vertical line with two horizontal lines extending from either side. The top of the vertical line indicates the highest price, and the bottom indicates the lowest price; the left horizontal line represents the opening price, and the right represents the closing price. This additional data provides a more comprehensive picture of price movements but can be overwhelming at first.

Candlestick charts are perhaps the most popular among traders, offering even more detailed information than bar charts. Each 'candlestick' on the chart shows the open, high, low, and close prices for a specific period, with the 'body' of the candlestick highlighting the range between the open and close prices. The 'wicks' or 'shadows' extending from the body represent the high and low prices. Candlestick charts not only display more information but also make it easier to identify patterns, which can be pivotal for decision-making.

As you get comfortable with the different types of charts, focus on understanding the timeframes they represent. Timeframes can range from as short as one minute to as long as a month. Shorter timeframes (like 1-minute or 5-minute charts) are generally favored by day traders looking to capitalize on small price movements. In contrast, longer timeframes (like daily or weekly charts) help swing traders and investors identify broader trends. For beginners, it is often advisable to start with longer timeframes to grasp the overall market sentiment before moving to shorter periods.

Analyzing trends is crucial when reading Forex charts. A trend indicates the general direction in which a currency pair's price is moving. There are three main types: uptrends, downtrends, and sideways trends. Uptrends are characterized by consistently higher highs and higher lows, signaling that buyers are in control. Downtrends show lower lows and lower highs, indicating that sellers dominate. Sideways trends, or range-bound markets, lack directional clarity and occur when prices move within a horizontal range.

One of the most effective ways to identify trends is by looking at moving averages. A moving average smooths out price data by creating a constantly updated average price over a specific period. Commonly used moving averages include the simple moving average (SMA) and the exponential moving average (EMA). While both provide valuable insights, the EMA gives more weight to recent prices, making it more responsive to new information. Plotting these on your chart helps you see the trend more clearly and can serve as a potential entry or exit signal.

Support and resistance levels are another key concept to understand when reading Forex charts. Support is a price level at which a currency pair tends to find buying interest, preventing the price from falling further. Resistance, on the other hand, is a level where selling interest is strong enough to prevent the price from rising further. Identifying these levels helps traders make decisions about where to enter or exit trades. Often, these levels can be identified by looking at historical price action, where the price has previously reversed directions.

Another important element to consider is price patterns. Price patterns are formations created by price movements and can signal future price action. Some commonly known patterns include head and shoulders, triangles, and double tops/bottoms. These patterns are used to predict market direction and help traders anticipate potential price movements. For instance, a head and shoulders pattern is typically seen as a reversal pattern, indicating that the previous trend is likely to change direction.

Volume is yet another essential aspect of reading Forex charts. Volume represents the number of transactions occurring in a market within a specified period. While Forex is a decentralized market and lacks a central exchange for accurate volume data, traders often use indicators like tick volume to gauge trading activity. Volume can confirm trends and patterns. A strong trend accompanied by high volume is more likely to continue, while one with low volume may lack the necessary strength.

Using technical indicators can also enhance your chart-reading skills. Technical indicators are calculations based on the price, volume, or open interest of a security. Common indicators include the Relative Strength Index (RSI), Moving Average Convergence Divergence (MACD), and Bollinger Bands. Each of these serves to provide additional information about market conditions and potential trading opportunities. For instance, the RSI helps identify overbought or oversold conditions, while MACD can signal potential trend reversals.

Combining different types of indicators can offer a more comprehensive analysis. For example, pairing moving averages with the RSI can help you not just see the trend but also gauge its strength and potential reversal points. Similarly, using Bollinger Bands alongside candlestick patterns might help identify potential breakout or breakdown levels. The key is to find a combination that works for your trading style and stick with it, refining as you gain more experience.

Finally, remember that reading Forex charts is both an art and a science. While the technical aspects are crucial, intuition plays a role too. The more you practice, the better you'll become at spotting opportunities and making informed decisions. Use demo accounts to practice without financial risk, and don't rush the learning process. Mastery over reading charts lays the foundation for more advanced trading strategies, moving you one step closer to becoming a proficient Forex trader.

Support and Resistance Levels

Support and Resistance Levels are a cornerstone of technical analysis in the Forex market, offering traders clear benchmarks to guide entry and exit points. Let's start by defining what these levels are. Support level is a price point where a currency pair tends to find support as it falls, meaning the price is more likely to bounce back up from this level rather than continue falling. Resistance level, on the other hand, is where the price tends to face a ceiling, likely resulting in a price fall rather than a continued rise. These levels are crucial as they offer a sort of map to understand price behavior, helping traders make informed decisions.

Understanding these levels might seem daunting at first, but they're essentially psychological barriers built on market sentiment. The more a price level is tested, the stronger it becomes as a support or resistance level. For instance, if a currency pair repeatedly drops to a particular price only to bounce back up, traders gain confidence that this price will likely serve as a dependable support level in the future. Similarly, if a currency pair keeps climbing to a certain price and then falling, that price becomes a notable resistance level.

Now, how do you identify these levels on a chart? It involves examining historical price action. By looking at past market movements, traders can pinpoint where the price has reversed multiple times. This can be done through simple observation or by using charting tools like horizontal lines in your trading platform. Often, these support and resistance levels align with round numbers or significant price levels, making them easier to spot.

There are various methods and tools traders use to identify these levels. One common method is the horizontal line, drawn at price levels where reversals have frequently occurred. Another approach is using moving averages, which can act as dynamic support or resistance levels. For instance, a 200-day moving average often serves as a strong support in an uptrend or resistance in a downtrend. More complex tools include Fibonacci retracements and pivot points, which are calculated based on previous price action and can provide more precise levels of support and resistance.

The concept of support and resistance doesn't stop at simply identifying these levels. It's also about understanding the potential for breakouts and breakdowns. A breakout occurs when the price moves above a resistance level, indicating the potential for further upward movement. Conversely, a breakdown happens when the price falls below a support level, signaling potential further declines. Recognizing these events can be just as important as the levels themselves, as they can indicate a shift in market dynamics and present trading opportunities.

Another vital aspect of support and resistance levels is knowing when they might fail. No support or resistance level is impenetrable. Market conditions such as news events, economic data releases, or changes in market sentiment can cause these levels to be breached. Therefore, it's crucial to remain vigilant and use other tools and indicators alongside to confirm price movements. For example, volume indicators can help ascertain the strength behind a breakout or breakdown, adding another layer of validation to your analysis.

Furthermore, support and resistance levels are not set in stone. As the market evolves, these levels can shift. What once was a resistance level can become a support level if the price breaks through it convincingly. This phenomenon, known as "role reversal," is common and highlights the dynamic nature of the Forex market. A former resistance level becomes a new line of support when the price persists above it, and vice versa.

Using support and resistance levels as part of your trading strategy requires practice and meticulous observation. Start by marking these levels on your charts and see how the price reacts to them. Combine this with other forms of technical analysis, such as trend lines and indicators, to build a comprehensive trading strategy. For instance, if a price is near a strong support level and there's a bullish trend, you might consider buying. Conversely, if the price is nearing resistance in a bearish trend, selling or shorting might be the prudent move.

Emotional discipline is crucial when trading with support and resistance levels. It's easy to get caught up in the excitement of a breakout or the fear of a breakdown. However, it's important to wait for confirmation. Experienced traders often wait for a retest of the broken level – for example, after a price breaks through resistance and then comes back to retest that level – before committing to a trade. This retest can serve as additional confirmation that the breakout or breakdown is genuine, reducing the likelihood of a false signal.

Integrating support and resistance levels into your trading routine also involves understanding their limitations. They are not foolproof predictors of future price action but rather guidelines based on historical behavior. This distinction is crucial because it fosters a mindset of caution and flexibility. Always be prepared to adjust your analysis as new price data becomes available. The market is ever-changing, and rigidity can lead to missed opportunities or unnecessary losses.

Furthermore, combining support and resistance analysis with fundamental aspects of Forex trading can yield even better results. For example, if an impending economic announcement is expected to be positive for a currency, and the price is approaching a strong support level, the likelihood of a bounce increases. Integrating both technical and fundamental analysis provides a holistic approach to understanding and navigating the Forex market.

Beyond identification and usage, documenting your findings on support and resistance levels can enhance your learning curve. Keeping a trading journal where you record instances of support and resistance interactions with the price can be highly beneficial. Over time, you'll recognize patterns and develop insights that can sharpen your trading acumen. Reviewing these journal entries can also provide invaluable lessons during periods of market volatility, helping you adapt and refine your strategies.

Support and resistance levels form the bedrock of many trading strategies, and mastering them can significantly enhance your trading performance. They offer a clear framework within which you can plan your trades, providing a set of reference points that simplify decision-making. Remember, successful trading is not about predicting markets with unerring accuracy but about managing probabilities and risks effectively. By integrating support and resistance levels into this broader strategy, you're building a robust foundation for consistent, thoughtful trading in the Forex market.

Trend Lines and Price Patterns

Trend Lines and Price Patterns are cornerstones of technical analysis, essential tools that offer insights into market behavior, helping traders identify potential price movements and make informed trading decisions. Understanding how to draw and interpret trend lines along with recognizing common price patterns is crucial for anyone looking to excel in Forex trading. By mastering these concepts, you'll be better equipped to anticipate market shifts and adjust your strategies accordingly.

Trend lines are essentially diagonal lines drawn on a price chart to connect specific data points, typically the highest highs or lowest lows. These lines help to visually represent the direction of the market—whether it's trending upward, downward, or moving sideways. An uptrend line connects consecutive higher lows, highlighting a bullish market where demand outpaces supply. Conversely, a downtrend line links successive lower highs, indicating a bearish market dominated by supply over demand.

To draw an effective trend line, you'll need at least two or more high or low points. The more points a trend line connects, the stronger the trend it signifies. However, it's imperative to remember that no trend lasts forever. Markets are inherently dynamic, and staying vigilant to potential trend reversals is part of smart trading.

Beyond their simplicity, trend lines serve as psychological barriers, where support and resistance become evident. In an uptrend, the trend line acts as a support level—indicating zones where buying interest resurfaces. In a downtrend, this line serves as a resistance zone suggesting selling pressure. The intersection of the price with trend lines often signals pivotal moments, leading to strategic opportunities for traders in the form of entries or exits.

While trend lines provide a solid framework, price patterns reveal the subtleties of market sentiment. Price patterns are formations created by the movement of the currency pairs, and they tend to signal potential market reversals or trends. Among the myriad patterns, several stand out due to their reliability and frequent occurrence.

One of the most well-known patterns is the *Head and Shoulders* pattern, often indicating a reversal in the prevailing trend. It consists of three peaks: the middle peak (the head) is higher than the two flanking peaks (the shoulders). This pattern typically forms at the end of an uptrend, signaling a transition to a downtrend. Conversely, the *Inverse Head and Shoulders* pattern suggests an impending upward movement when spotted at the end of a downtrend.

Another vital pattern to understand is the *Double Top and Double Bottom*. The Double Top marks a bullish-to-bearish reversal, shaped by two peaks at a similar price level followed by a breakout downward. On the flip side, the Double Bottom indicates a bearish-to-bullish reversal, created by two troughs at a comparable price level followed by an upward breakout.

Triangles are also common, coming in three variants— ascending, descending, and symmetrical. Ascending triangles typically form in an uptrend and signal a continuation of bullish momentum. Descending triangles appear in downtrends and suggest further bearish movement. Symmetrical triangles, characterized by converging trend lines, can form in either up or down markets, suggesting a potential breakout in either direction.

Flags and pennants serve as short-term continuation patterns, usually emerging after a robust price movement. These patterns are characterized by a brief consolidation phase marked by small fluctuations, followed by a resumption of the prior trend. Flags are rectangular, while pennants take the shape of small symmetrical triangles.

It's essential to note that while patterns and trend lines are powerful, they should never be used in isolation. Always consider the broader market context and incorporate other technical indicators to validate your predictions. Indicators like Moving Averages, Relative Strength Index (RSI), and MACD can complement your analysis, offering additional layers of confirmation and reducing the risk of false signals.

In addition, keep an eye on the volume accompanying these patterns. High volume often confirms the strength of a pattern or trend line breakout. For instance, in a triangle pattern, a significant volume spike during the breakout phase signals increased interest among traders, lending more credibility to the pattern.

An essential aspect of mastering trend lines and price patterns lies in continual practice and observation. The more you chart and analyze these elements in real-time conditions, the more proficient you'll become in quicker identification and response. Harnessing tools such as demo accounts can offer a risk-free environment to refine these skills before transitioning to live trading.

Remember, Forex trading is both an art and a science. While technical analysis provides a systematic and consistent approach, there's an element of intuition that develops over time. Observing past chart behaviors, noting how patterns played out, and learning from missteps will gradually sharpen your analytical skills and decision-making prowess.

Incorporating these techniques into your trading strategy can significantly enhance your market insights, thus improving your ability to identify profitable trades. However, it's crucial to maintain emotional discipline and not make impulsive decisions based solely on pattern recognition. Balancing analysis with a sound risk management plan is the key to long-term success.

To sum it up, **Trend Lines and Price Patterns** are indispensable tools in your Forex trading toolkit. They help in demystifying market movements, enabling you to make educated trading decisions. With practice and persistence, you'll be able to leverage these tools to read the market effectively, minimize risks, and maximize gains on your Forex trading journey.

CHAPTER 5:
DEVELOPING A TRADING STRATEGY

A s you dive deeper into the realm of Forex trading, developing a robust trading strategy becomes crucial for success. A well-crafted trading strategy isn't just a set of arbitrary guidelines; it's a tailored blueprint that aligns with your financial goals, risk appetite, and market insights. This chapter will empower you to discern between different types of trading strategies and guide you through creating a personal trading plan that reflects your unique perspective. Additionally, we'll delve into the importance of backtesting your strategy to ensure its viability before you risk real capital. This grounding in strategy development will help you build the confidence needed to navigate the Forex market, giving you the tools to make informed and strategic trading decisions.

Types of Trading Strategies

Types of Trading Strategies serve as the backbone to any successful trader's toolkit, especially for those of you who are just diving into the multifaceted world of currency trading. Understanding the various trading strategies can empower you to make more informed decisions, helping you to navigate through the complexities of the Forex market with a bit more ease and confidence.

First off, it's essential to grasp that no single trading strategy fits all scenarios. Markets are dynamic, and what works in one situation might not work in another. However, certain well-established strategies have stood the test of time and continue to offer substantial value to traders of all levels. Let's explore some of the cornerstone strategies you can consider integrating into your trading plan.

One of the first strategies that you'll come across is *Scalping*. Scalping involves making dozens or even hundreds of trades in a single day, aiming to 'scalp' small profits from each trade. The key to scalping is speed. Trades are typically held for just a few seconds or minutes. Because of the rapid pace, scalping requires a high degree of discipline and quick decision-making skills. Scalpers need to be lightning-fast in executing their trades and must constantly monitor the markets to identify fleeting opportunities.

On the other side of the spectrum, there is *Day Trading*. Unlike scalping, day trading involves making trades that are executed within a single trading day, but not held overnight. Day traders aim to take advantage of short-term market movements by identifying trends within the trading day. While this strategy doesn't require the same level of speed as scalping, it does necessitate a thorough understanding of market behavior and strong analytical skills. Day trading allows for more time to make trading decisions but also requires a significant time commitment to monitor the markets throughout the day.

Then, we have *Swing Trading*. This strategy sits in the middle ground between day trading and long-term investing. Swing traders look to capture gains from market swings that occur over a few days to several weeks. They rely heavily on technical analysis and are less concerned with the minute-by-minute movements that scalpers and day traders focus on. This strategy allows for more flexibility and is ideal for those who cannot commit to monitoring the markets all day but still want to benefit from market volatility.

Position Trading is another key strategy and often involves holding trades for several weeks, months, or even years. Position traders rely on fundamental analysis to identify long-term trends and investment opportunities. They are less concerned with short-term fluctuations and focus on the broader economic and market outlook. This strategy requires a significant amount of patience and a strong understanding of macroeconomic factors. Position traders can benefit from large market movements and trends but must be able to tolerate extended periods of market fluctuations.

Moving into more specialized strategies, *Trend Trading* is quite popular. Trend traders aim to capitalize on market momentum by identifying and following prevailing trends. They use various technical indicators and chart patterns to determine the direction of the market. When a new trend is identified, trend traders will enter trades in the direction of the trend and hold their position until the trend shows signs of reversal. This strategy requires a good grasp of technical analysis and is effective in markets that exhibit clear trending behavior.

Counter-Trend Trading, or mean reversion trading, takes an opposite approach. Counter-trend traders look to exploit short-term reversals within a prevailing trend. They believe that markets often overextend and eventually revert to a mean value. This strategy involves identifying overbought or oversold conditions and entering trades in the opposite direction of the prevailing trend. While this strategy can be profitable, it carries higher risk as it goes against the main market trend. Proper risk management is crucial to mitigate potential losses.

News-Based Trading is another exciting strategy. Here, traders speculate on market movements based on news releases and economic data. These can include employment reports, GDP figures, central bank announcements, and other significant events. News-based traders must be well-informed and able to react quickly to new information. This strategy can lead to substantial profits, especially during periods of high volatility, but can also be risky due to the unpredictability of the markets' reactions to news events.

You might also encounter strategies based on *Technical Indicators*, such as moving averages, Relative Strength Index (RSI), and Bollinger Bands. These tools help traders identify potential entry and exit points based on historical price data and mathematical calculations. Technical indicators can be used independently or in combination with other trading strategies to enhance decision-making. Mastering these tools requires practice and a good understanding of how they reflect market psychology.

Lastly, let's not overlook *Automated Trading Systems*, otherwise known as algorithmic trading or bots. These systems use pre-programmed rules to execute trades automatically. The algorithms can be designed to follow a specific strategy, from trend-following to arbitrage. Automated trading removes emotional biases and allows for rapid execution of trades. However, it's essential to thoroughly backtest and optimize these systems to ensure they are effective in various market conditions.

As you navigate through these strategies, remember that the most successful traders often combine elements from multiple strategies to develop a personalized approach that suits their individual risk tolerance, time commitment, and market understanding. Experiment with different strategies using demo accounts initially and analyze what works best for you. The goal is to build a robust trading plan that can adapt to changing market conditions and helps you achieve consistent success over time.

Knowledge is power, especially in the Forex market. With a solid understanding of various trading strategies, you are better equipped to face the challenges and seize the opportunities that come your way. Stay disciplined, remain curious, and never stop learning. The journey to becoming a successful trader may be arduous, but the rewards can be well worth the effort.

Creating Your Personal Trading Plan

Creating Your Personal Trading Plan is more than just a step in your Forex journey—it's your roadmap to success. Like any journey, having a clear plan helps you avoid mistakes, stay focused, and manage your risks effectively. This section will guide you through the essential elements of constructing a trading plan that aligns with your goals, personality, and risk tolerance.

First, let's clarify what we mean by a trading plan. A trading plan is a comprehensive, well-thought-out written document that outlines your trading goals, strategies, risk management rules, and evaluation criteria. It's not just about making money; it's about creating a disciplined approach to trading that can foster consistent, sustainable growth.

Your trading plan should start with your *financial goals*. These goals need to be specific, measurable, achievable, relevant, and time-bound (SMART). Are you aiming to double your account within a year? Or perhaps, you simply want a steady monthly return of 2-5%. Knowing where you want to go is the first step in figuring out how to get there.

Next, you'll want to define your *trading style*, which should suit your lifestyle and personality. Are you a day trader who thrives on quick decisions and action-packed days? Or a swing trader who's more comfortable holding positions for several days or weeks, allowing for more thoughtful decision-making? Your trading style will dictate how often you trade, the strategies you employ, and even the markets you choose to participate in.

Once you've pinpointed your trading style, you'll need to establish your *risk tolerance*. How much of your capital are you willing to risk on a single trade? This is typically expressed as a percentage of your trading account. A common rule of thumb is the 1-2% rule, where you risk no more than 1-2% of your account on any given trade. Understanding your risk tolerance helps you to manage your emotions and remain level-headed, even when the market is volatile.

With your goals, trading style, and risk tolerance in place, you can move on to outlining your *trading strategies*. This includes both technical and fundamental analysis methods that you'll use to identify trading opportunities. For example, if you're a technical trader, you might focus on trend lines, moving averages, and candlestick patterns. If you lean towards fundamental analysis, economic indicators like GDP, employment data, and interest rate decisions may be more up your alley. Whatever your preference, make sure to document the specific criteria that must be met for you to enter and exit trades.

Your trading plan should also detail your *risk management rules*. This includes setting stop-loss and take-profit levels to protect your capital and lock in gains. It's crucial to stick to these rules rigorously; deviating from them can lead to emotional trading, which is often a recipe for disaster. Make it a habit to review and adjust these rules periodically as your experience grows and market conditions change.

Evaluation and continuous improvement are also key components of your trading plan. Set aside time regularly to *review your trades* and assess whether you're meeting your goals. Were your trades successful? Did they follow your plan? If not, what went wrong? Keeping a trading journal can be an invaluable tool in this process, as it allows you to track your performance over time, identify patterns, and make informed adjustments.

Incorporate *contingency plans* in your trading plan. Markets can be unpredictable, and black swan events can occur unexpectedly. Have a plan for these scenarios. Whether it's setting a maximum drawdown limit or having a 'circuit breaker' rule to stop trading for the day after a series of losses, these measures can protect you from catastrophic losses.

Let's not forget the importance of *psychological preparedness*. Trading can be emotionally taxing, and it's essential to mentally prepare yourself for both wins and losses. Techniques like mindfulness, meditation, or even consulting with a trading coach can help you stay focused and disciplined. Remember, the goal is to make trading decisions based on logic and data, not emotions.

Your trading plan should be a living document—something you revisit and refine continually. As you gain more experience and learn from your trades, you'll find areas that need tweaking. Perhaps your risk tolerance has changed, or you've discovered a new indicator that significantly enhances your strategy. Being flexible and open to improvements will make you a more adaptive and successful trader over time.

Lastly, don't underestimate the value of *community and mentorship*. Join forums, attend webinars, or even find a mentor who has been in the trenches. You can learn a lot from the experiences of others, which can help you avoid common pitfalls and accelerate your learning curve.

Your comprehensive trading plan is the cornerstone of your Forex trading journey. By clearly defining your goals, strategies, risk management rules, and evaluation criteria, you create a disciplined and structured approach that enhances your chances of success. Remember, it's a journey of constant learning and improvement, and your trading plan is your most reliable guide along the way.

Backtesting Your Strategy

Backtesting Your Strategy is a crucial step in developing a robust Forex trading plan. At its core, backtesting involves applying your trading strategy to historical market data to evaluate its effectiveness. This process helps you gauge how your strategy would have performed in the past, offering insights into potential future performance. By meticulously analyzing past data, you can identify strengths and weaknesses in your strategy, fine-tune it, and gain the confidence needed to employ it in live trading.

Backtesting isn't just about number crunching; it's a holistic approach that requires a blend of technical knowledge, analytical skills, and patience. Imagine you have designed a strategy that looks promising on paper. The real challenge lies in verifying whether it holds up under various market conditions that have occurred in the past. Through backtesting, you can simulate trades over a specified period and scrutinize if the strategy yields consistent results or if it needs further adjustments.

One of the first steps in backtesting is gathering historical data relevant to your chosen currency pairs. This data can often be sourced from your trading platform or third-party providers. It's essential to ensure that the data is of high quality, free from errors, and encompasses a broad timeframe. Having a comprehensive dataset allows you to test your strategy across different market cycles, including bull markets, bear markets, and periods of high volatility.

The actual process of backtesting involves using software tools to automate the application of your strategy to historical data. Many trading platforms come equipped with built-in backtesting capabilities. Tools like MetaTrader, NinjaTrader, and TradingView provide user-friendly interfaces where you can input your strategy parameters and run tests. Alternatively, more advanced traders might prefer coding custom backtesting scripts in languages like Python, R, or MATLAB for greater flexibility and precision.

Let's not overlook the importance of setting up your backtest correctly. The parameters you choose can significantly influence the results. Make sure to specify your entry and exit rules clearly, define your stop-loss and take-profit levels, and account for any transaction costs or slippage. Remember, the goal isn't to achieve unrealistic perfection but to ensure your strategy is viable under real-world conditions.

Interpreting backtest results is an art that combines data analysis and financial acumen. Look beyond the raw profit figures. Pay attention to key performance metrics like the maximum drawdown, the win/loss ratio, the Sharpe ratio, and the profit factor. These metrics help you understand the risk and reward characteristics of your strategy. A strategy that shows steady returns with minimal drawdowns might be more desirable than one that achieves high profits sporadically but undergoes large drawdowns.

Another vital aspect of backtesting is the concept of data snooping. It's easy to fall into the trap of cherry-picking data that supports your strategy while ignoring periods where performance faltered. To avoid this, consider splitting your data into an in-sample set for optimization and an out-sample set for validation. This method helps ensure that your strategy is genuinely robust and not overfitted to specific historical conditions.

Sometimes, the insights gained from backtesting might reveal that your strategy requires tweaks. Don't be disheartened if initial results are less than stellar. Use these insights constructively to improve your strategy. Maybe your entry signals are too aggressive, or perhaps your risk management rules need tightening. The iterative process of refining and re-testing can turn a mediocre strategy into a profitable one.

- Identifying patterns and anomalies

- Testing different market conditions

- Refining entry and exit points

Realizing that backtesting is a continual process is crucial. Markets evolve, and a strategy that worked wonders five years ago might not be as effective today. Regularly revisit your backtests, update your data, and fine-tune your strategy as necessary. This ongoing process ensures that you remain adaptive and resilient in the face of changing market dynamics.

A critical yet often overlooked component of backtesting is stress testing. Beyond regular backtesting, subject your strategy to extreme market conditions to gauge its robustness. What happens to your strategy during unexpected market crashes or unprecedented bull runs? Stress testing prepares you for outlier events that could significantly impact your trading performance and allows you to adjust your risk management parameters accordingly.

Finally, while backtesting is invaluable, it's not infallible. Historical performance is not always indicative of future results. Markets are influenced by myriad factors, and unexpected events can still throw even the best strategies off course. Therefore, consider backtesting as one piece of the puzzle. Combine it with forward testing in a demo account to observe how your strategy performs in current market conditions without risking real capital.

In conclusion, mastering the art of backtesting can significantly enhance your Forex trading journey. It provides a scientific foundation for your trading decisions and cultivates a deeper understanding of market behaviors. Although it demands effort and attention to detail, the rewards can be substantial. By investing time in backtesting, you're not just testing a strategy; you're building a pathway to informed, confident, and potentially profitable trading.

CHAPTER 6:
THE PSYCHOLOGY OF TRADING

Understanding the psychology of trading is essential for anyone serious about success in the Forex market. Emotional discipline acts as the backbone of insightful decision-making, often separating profitable trades from costly errors. It's crucial to recognize and manage emotions like fear and greed that can cloud judgment and lead to impulsive actions. Overcoming these emotional hurdles requires not just theoretical knowledge but practical, consistent effort. Developing patience is equally vital, as waiting for the right opportunities and adhering to a well-formulated plan significantly enhances one's chances of achieving long-term profitability. Mastering the psychological aspects of trading is not a one-time feat but a continual journey of self-awareness and improvement, arming you with the mental fortitude to navigate the highs and lows of the Forex market confidently.

Emotional Discipline

Emotional Discipline plays a crucial role in the realm of Forex trading, especially for newcomers who are still finding their footing. Understanding market trends, reading charts, and devising strategies are integral parts of the trading process, but none of these skills will be effective without the ability to maintain emotional control. Emotional discipline is all about managing your emotional reactions to market movements, whether they're in your favor or against you. Maintaining this control can mean the difference between a successful trader and one who continually incurs losses.

One of the first aspects of emotional discipline is recognizing emotional triggers. For example, it's common to feel a rush of excitement when a trade initially moves in your favor. However, this excitement can turn to anxiety if the market begins to reverse. Without emotional discipline, traders might impulsively adjust their strategies based on fleeting feelings, leading to poor decision-making. It's vital to stay level-headed and stick to your trading plan, even when your instincts are pushing you to react.

Another key element in emotional discipline involves setting realistic expectations. Forex trading isn't a get-rich-quick scheme. Recognizing that losses are part of the trading landscape will prepare you emotionally for the bumps along the way. Accepting that losing trades are inevitable allows you to focus on long-term success rather than short-term wins and losses. Traders with this mindset are better equipped to persevere through challenges without making impulsive decisions.

Developing emotional resilience is equally important. The market can be unpredictable, and even well-researched trades can go against you. Emotional resilience means having the ability to bounce back from losses and continue trading with a clear mind. One effective practice is to engage in regular self-reflection and meditation to manage stress levels. Taking breaks and disconnecting from trading during heavy market turbulence can also help maintain emotional balance.

Equally important is avoiding the influence of external noise. In the Forex market, news events and opinions can create panic or euphoria. Traders need to build the ability to filter out noise and base their decisions on solid analysis and their trading plan. Consistently second-guessing yourself due to external opinions can lead to erratic trading behavior and underperformance.

One practical approach is to utilize automated systems and tools to mitigate emotional influences. Automated trading strategies are designed to execute trades based on predefined criteria, removing the emotional component altogether. While these systems aren't foolproof, they can significantly reduce the chances of making emotionally-driven decisions. Using stop-loss orders can also provide a safeguard against emotional reactions, ensuring that losses are cut before they become unmanageable.

Let's not forget the substantial impact of journaling. Keeping a detailed trading journal allows you to track not only your trades but also your emotional states during those trades. By documenting your thought processes and feelings, you can identify recurring emotional triggers and develop strategies to manage them. Over time, this practice can help you become more emotionally disciplined, improving your decision-making and trading outcomes.

Accountability is another method to enhance emotional discipline. Engaging with a trading mentor or joining a trading community can provide external support and perspective. Sharing your trades and strategies with others can enforce a stricter adherence to your trading plan since there's a level of accountability involved. These external checks can encourage you to act more rationally rather than emotionally.

Incorporating emotional discipline into your trading routine won't happen overnight, but committing to it can significantly improve your trading performance. Building this discipline involves continuous learning and adaptation. As you progress in your trading journey, regularly revisit your trading plan and emotional management strategies to tweak and improve upon them.

Finally, balance in life is essential for emotional discipline. Ensure you're getting enough rest, exercise, and personal time away from the screens. A healthy body supports a healthy mind, which in turn promotes better emotional control. Staying well-rounded helps keep your emotional responses in check and contributes to long-term trading success.

Overcoming Fear and Greed

Overcoming Fear and Greed is often the most challenging aspect of Forex trading, particularly for beginners. These two emotions can wreak havoc on your trading decisions, leading to significant losses even when you have a solid strategy in place. Understanding the role that fear and greed play in your trading psychology is the first step toward mastering them.

Fear in trading usually manifests as hesitation to enter a trade, panic when a trade goes against you, or the premature closing of a profitable position. Greed often appears as the desire to hold onto a winning trade for too long, increasing your risk exposure in the hopes of making even more profit. Both emotions are natural human responses, but if allowed to dominate your trading decisions, they can lead to catastrophic outcomes.

To overcome fear, you must first recognize it. This could mean journaling your thoughts and emotions when you trade. By identifying patterns, you'll learn to see when fear is influencing your decisions. One effective way to deal with fear is to adopt a systematic approach to decision-making. Leveraging tools like stop-loss orders and employing a well-structured trading plan can help mitigate the impact of fear. When you trust your strategy, you're less likely to make impulsive decisions driven by emotion.

On the flip side, greed can be equally destructive. A common manifestation of greed is overtrading, where you take more trades than your strategy dictates, often based on the mistaken belief that recent success can be easily replicated. The first step in overcoming greed is setting realistic profit targets. Defining what success looks like for each trade helps you avoid the temptation to go for the home run, risking more than necessary.

A useful tactic to keep greed in check is to have predefined take-profit points. Much like stop-loss orders for managing fear, take-profit points allow you to bank gains systematically and remove the emotional drive to "let it ride." Combined with a robust trading journal, these can provide a framework for reflecting on your trading behavior and its adherence to your strategy.

Some traders find it helpful to implement a documented trading plan that includes specific rules for entry and exit. This plan can act as a guide, especially during emotional times. Clearly defined criteria make it easier to stick to your strategy and resist the urge to make trades based on gut feelings or emotional highs.

Another significant part of overcoming fear and greed is risk management. Allocating only a small proportion of your trading capital to each trade can limit your exposure to loss, thereby reducing fear. Effective risk management strategies, like the 1% rule, ensure that no single trade can significantly impact your overall capital, giving you the psychological comfort to trade without excessive fear or greed.

Understanding market conditions also plays a vital role in managing these emotions. Market volatility can amplify emotions, making it crucial to be aware of the current market climate. During times of higher volatility, it might be wise to trade smaller positions or abstain from trading altogether to avoid emotional roller coasters.

Mindfulness and mental conditioning are also essential for overcoming fear and greed. Techniques such as meditation and mindfulness can help you remain present and focused, enabling you to make more rational decisions. Regularly practicing these techniques can build emotional resilience and improve your overall trading mindset.

Furthermore, external support can be invaluable. Participating in trader forums, joining trading communities, or even seeking mentorship from experienced traders can provide the encouragement and validation required to stick to your plan during tough times. Shared experiences and collective wisdom often offer new perspectives and coping strategies that you might not have considered.

Education is another critical component. The more you understand about the market, the less likely you'll be swayed by fear or greed. Continuous learning through courses, books, and webinars can provide deeper insights into market behaviors, equipping you with the knowledge to navigate volatility more confidently.

Moreover, setting long-term goals rather than focusing solely on immediate returns can help temper greed. When your objective is sustainable growth over years rather than weeks or months, the lure of quick profits becomes less appealing. You'll be more inclined to follow your trading plan and stick to prudent risk management practices.

Last but not least, always remember that mistakes and losses are part of the trading journey. Accepting them as learning opportunities rather than failures reduces the fear of making trades. This acceptance also helps in preventing greed-driven decisions, as it shifts the focus from chasing profits to building a consistent and sustainable trading practice.

In conclusion, **Overcoming Fear and Greed** in Forex trading requires a blend of self-awareness, disciplined strategies, risk management, and continuous learning. By acknowledging these emotions and taking proactive steps to manage them, you'll be better equipped to make rational, informed trading decisions that align with your long-term financial goals. Building this psychological resilience not only optimizes your chances of success but also makes the trading journey more enjoyable and rewarding.

The Importance of Patience

The Importance of Patience can't be overstated for anyone venturing into the world of Forex trading. When you're just starting, it's easy to get swayed by the allure of quick profits and fast trades. However, the reality of trading is quite different. This market punishes haste and rewards those who are disciplined enough to wait for the right opportunities.

Think of patience as the foundation upon which your trading strategy is built. Without it, every other tool or technique you employ may crumble under the pressure of impulsive decisions. For beginners, this means resisting the urge to jump on every trade that looks promising at a glance. Markets are dynamic and often deceptive, presenting what appears to be golden opportunities that could, in fact, be traps. Patience allows you to filter out these false leads and act only on validated, high-probability setups.

In the initial stages of trading, it's crucial to take time to learn and absorb the basics thoroughly. Rushing through tutorials, skipping essential readings, or diving headfirst into live trading will not lead to sustained success. It's that slow and steady accumulation of knowledge, combined with practical experience, that will set you up for long-term profitability. Reflect on each trade, understand what worked and what didn't, and adjust accordingly. This reflective practice can only be nurtured through patience.

Patience also plays a critical role during live trades. Once you've set your trade, it's tempting to keep checking it constantly or second-guessing your strategy. This often leads to anxiety and emotional trading, which are the enemies of success. Trust your analysis and let the market unfold. Sometimes the best action is no action at all. Remember, you don't have to be in a trade all the time to be a successful trader. Waiting for the right moment is half the battle won.

When the market moves against your position, it's easy to panic and make haste decisions. Here, patience ties directly into emotional discipline. Staying calm, sticking to your original plan, and resisting the impulse to react to every fluctuation can save you from unnecessary losses. Emotions are powerful triggers, and they can easily dominate your trading behavior if you're not careful. Patience helps you manage these emotions and keeps you grounded, enabling you to make rational decisions.

Beyond the mechanics of individual trades, patience is essential in the broader perspective of your trading career. Building a profitable trading portfolio doesn't happen overnight. It requires consistent effort, a willingness to learn from mistakes, and an enduring commitment to your trading plan. Losses are inevitable, but they become learning opportunities when you're patient enough to analyze them and draw meaningful insights.

An important facet of patience is knowing when to exit a trade. Some traders fall victim to holding onto losing positions for too long, hoping the market will turn in their favor. Others may prematurely exit winning trades due to fear of losing profits. Both scenarios can be mitigated by patiently adhering to your predefined exit strategies, whether it's based on set profit targets or stop-loss levels. Patience ensures you stick to your plan without succumbing to market noise.

Moreover, market conditions are constantly evolving. A strategy that works today might not be effective tomorrow. Patience during these transitions allows you to avoid knee-jerk reactions that could derail your overall objectives. Instead of switching strategies on a whim, give them time to play out fully. This approach not only tests the robustness of your strategy but also enhances your adaptability—a critical skill in Forex trading.

On a larger time frame, growing your account balance requires patience. Many new traders fall into the trap of aiming for high returns in a short period. This mindset often leads to risky behaviors such as over-leveraging and taking unnecessary risks. Instead, focus on steady, incremental gains. Compounding these gains over time is where true wealth in Forex trading is built. Patience ensures you don't take on risks that could wipe out your account.

It's also worth mentioning the value of patience in ongoing education. The currency market is vast and complex. Seasoned traders understand the importance of continual learning—whether it's new trading techniques, market insights, or psychological resilience. Patience in learning and evolving your trading approach gives you an edge over those who rely solely on past knowledge and rigid tactics.

Even when it comes to implementing new strategies, patience is your ally. Backtesting, for example, requires rigorous data analysis over extended periods. Being patient enough to thoroughly test and validate strategies before putting them to use in a live market can save you from costly mistakes. This disciplined approach enables you to enter the market with greater confidence and a higher probability of success.

Lastly, patience cultivates a professional mindset. When you view trading as a business rather than a get-rich-quick scheme, you're more likely to approach it with the seriousness and dedication it requires. Successful traders have long understood that Forex trading is a journey. They invest time in understanding market dynamics, refining their strategies, and developing their mental fortitude. Emulating this approach sets you on a path to becoming a proficient trader.

So, embrace patience in every aspect of your trading journey. Whether it's during the learning phase, while executing trades, in managing your emotions, or even in adapting to new market realities, patience can be your most crucial asset. Remember, the goal is sustained profitability and growth. And that achievement, without a doubt, is built on a bedrock of patience.

CHAPTER 7:
RISK MANAGEMENT TECHNIQUES

Risk management isn't just about protecting your capital; it's the backbone of successful trading. Effective risk management techniques help you survive in the volatile world of Forex, where even the most experienced traders face unpredictable markets. You need to set stop loss and take profit levels to guard against significant losses and lock in gains. Managing your leverage and margin meticulously ensures you don't overextend yourself, while the 1% Risk Rule is a golden principle that limits your exposure on any single trade to a manageable fraction of your account. By incorporating these techniques, you build a safety net that allows you to trade with confidence, knowing you're prepared for the inevitable ups and downs. Remember, it's not about eliminating risk but about controlling it smartly.

Setting Stop Loss and Take Profit

Setting Stop Loss and Take Profit is a fundamental aspect of risk management in Forex trading. These tools help traders manage their trades efficiently by automating exit points, thus safeguarding their capital and locking in profits. While setting stop loss and take profit levels may seem straightforward, understanding their nuances and implementing them effectively can significantly enhance your trading performance.

Let's begin by defining what stop loss and take profit are. Simply put, a stop loss is an order placed to sell a security when it reaches a certain price, limiting the trader's loss on a position. Conversely, a take profit order is set to sell a security when it hits a certain price, ensuring that profits are locked in when the market moves in a favorable direction.

So, why are these tools so crucial? The forex market can be extremely volatile, and prices can swing dramatically within short periods. Without stop losses and take profits, you expose your trades to the whims of the market, which can wipe out your capital swiftly. By using these tools, you establish predefined exit points that automate your trading strategy, allowing for disciplined trading.

When placing a stop loss, the primary goal is to determine a level at which the trade will be closed to prevent further losses. Generally, the stop loss level should be based on your risk tolerance and the market's volatility. For instance, placing a stop loss too close to the entry point in a highly volatile market might trigger an unnecessary exit if minor fluctuations occur. Conversely, setting it too far might result in significant losses.

One common approach to setting stop loss levels is using technical analysis. For example, you might place a stop loss just below a key support level if you're buying a currency pair. If the price falls below this level, it might indicate that the market sentiment has shifted, and it's time to exit the trade. Additionally, it's crucial to consider the Average True Range (ATR) indicator, which helps gauge market volatility and set appropriate stop loss levels.

Another consideration when setting stop losses is the size of your trade, often referred to as position sizing. The size of your trade should be determined based on your overall account balance and the amount you're willing to risk on a single trade. A commonly followed rule is the 1% risk rule, which we'll discuss in more detail in another section. By carefully calculating position sizes, you ensure that even if your stop loss is hit, your financial risk remains manageable.

On the flip side, take profit levels are equally important. These levels help you lock in gains when the market moves in your favor. Similar to stop losses, take profit levels can be determined using technical indicators such as resistance levels. For example, if you're selling a currency pair, you might set your take profit just above a key resistance level, anticipating that the price will struggle to break through this barrier.

However, be mindful of the risk-to-reward ratio when setting your take profit levels. The risk-to-reward ratio compares the potential loss (risk) of a trade to the potential profit (reward). A commonly recommended ratio is 1:2, meaning that your potential profit should be at least twice your potential loss. This balanced approach ensures that even if you have more losing trades than winning ones, your overall profitability can remain positive.

Psychologically, having predefined stop losses and take profits can alleviate some emotional stress associated with trading. Decisions made on the fly are often influenced by fear and greed, which can lead to suboptimal outcomes. By setting these levels in advance, you create a structured plan that can prevent impulsive decisions.

It's also worth mentioning the trailing stop order, a dynamic tool that adjusts your stop loss level as the market moves in your favor. A trailing stop follows the market price at a fixed distance. For instance, if you set a trailing stop at 20 pips, it will move up 20 pips for every 20-pip increase in the market price. This allows you to lock in profits while giving your trade room to breathe.

Let's consider a practical example to bring these concepts to life. Suppose you enter a long position on EUR/USD at 1.2000. Based on your analysis, you anticipate that the price could rise to 1.2100, but you're also aware of significant support at 1.1950. Therefore, you set your stop loss at 1.1950, just below this support level, and your take profit at 1.2100. This setup has a risk-to-reward ratio of 1:2, aligning with sound risk management practices.

As the trade progresses, the market begins to move in your favor, and the price reaches 1.2050. Rather than manually adjusting your stop loss, you decide to use a trailing stop of 50 pips. Now, if the price rises further to 1.2100, your stop loss will automatically move to 1.2050, ensuring you retain some profits even if the market reverses.

Consistency in applying stop loss and take profit strategies can significantly impact your trading success. It's tempting to adjust these levels based on your emotions, especially when a trade isn't going as planned. However, sticking to your predefined levels fosters discipline and consistency, ultimately leading to better long-term results.

Moreover, backtesting your strategy can provide valuable insights into the effectiveness of your stop loss and take profit settings. By using historical data to simulate your trading strategy, you can assess how your predefined levels would have performed under various market conditions. This process can help you refine your approach and make necessary adjustments to improve your strategy's performance.

Of course, no strategy is foolproof, and it's essential to remain flexible and adapt to changing market conditions. Sometimes, a news event or an unexpected market move can prompt you to manually adjust your stop loss or take profit levels. However, such adjustments should be made strategically, not impulsively, to ensure they align with your overall risk management plan.

In conclusion, **Setting Stop Loss and Take Profit** is indispensable for effective Forex trading. By automating your exit points, you manage risk more effectively and lock in profits systematically. While it requires careful consideration and planning, mastering these tools can empower you to navigate the Forex market with greater confidence and discipline. Remember, consistent application and continual refinement are key to building a resilient trading strategy that stands the test of time.

Managing Leverage and Margin

Managing Leverage and Margin is a key skill set that every aspiring Forex trader must grasp to trade effectively and safeguard their investments. Leverage, often called a double-edged sword, allows traders to control larger positions with a relatively small amount of capital. This can amplify gains but also magnify losses. Margin, on the other hand, is the collateral required by your broker to cover potential losses. Understanding how to manage both can mean the difference between flourishing in the Forex market or facing significant financial setbacks.

Leverage essentially allows you to borrow money from your broker to increase the size of your trade beyond what your account balance would usually allow. Most brokers offer leverage ratios like 50:1, 100:1, or even 500:1, which means you can control $50,000 with just $1,000 if you leverage at 50:1. This can be extremely beneficial if the market moves in your favor, as your potential profit is multiplied. But be warned, the same applies to losses.

Let's break it down with an example. Say you only have $1,000 but want to trade $50,000 worth of a currency pair. With a leverage ratio of 50:1, this is possible. If the market moves 1% in your favor, you make 1% of $50,000, which is $500. Conversely, if it moves against you by 1%, you lose $500. That's half your initial deposit gone in just a tiny market move.

The temptation with leverage is to go for higher ratios, thinking that larger trades will result in greater profits. While that's true, the risks also skyrocket. This is where responsible leverage management comes into play. The golden rule is to use leverage conservatively. Think twice, maybe even thrice, before opting for higher leverage ratios, especially if you're new to Forex trading.

Margin, on the flip side, acts as security for your leveraged trade. When you open a leveraged position, a portion of your account balance is set aside by the broker as margin. This ensures that you can cover potential losses. If your trade goes against you, and your losses exceed the margin, you may get a margin call from your broker. This is essentially a warning that you need to deposit more funds to keep your position open. If you can't, your broker may close your position to limit further losses.

Maintaining a healthy margin level is critical. One way to do this is by keeping an eye on the "margin level" percentage in your trading platform, which is usually calculated as (Equity/Margin) * 100. A margin level of below 100% usually triggers a margin call. To stay safe, aim to keep your margin level well above this threshold.

Another tactic is to use stop-loss orders religiously. A stop-loss order can automatically close your position at a pre-determined level, securing your remaining capital. This simple tool can save you from reaching a margin call scenario. You don't need to monitor your trades constantly if you have a solid stop-loss strategy in place.

Risk management is always interconnected with leverage and margin. The general advice for beginners is to risk no more than 1-2% of your trading capital on a single trade. This ensures that even if several trades go wrong consecutively, your account balance remains robust, allowing you to stay in the game longer.

Leverage and margin should work as tools to enhance your trading prospects, not as pitfalls waiting to snare the unwary. With careful planning and a disciplined approach, they can bolster your trading strategy, enabling you to capitalize on market opportunities while still preserving your capital. The journey might seem daunting initially, but by respecting the risks and leveraging prudently, you'll find a sustainable path in Forex trading.

Also, it's crucial to align your leverage and margin use with your overall trading strategy. For instance, day traders might use different leverage settings compared to swing traders. Day traders often seek multiple small gains throughout the day and might use slightly higher leverage given their shorter holding periods. Swing traders, who hold positions over several days or weeks, generally benefit from more conservative leverage, providing a cushion against weekend gaps and extended market volatility.

Always remember to revisit and review your leverage and margin strategies regularly. As your trading experience grows, you might find the need to adjust your leverage based on market conditions and your evolving risk tolerance. Educational resources, webinars, and continual learning will also help you stay updated with best practices in managing leverage and margin.

Your broker's platform will usually provide tools and indicators to monitor leverage and margin levels. Utilize them to keep track of your trading activity. Being consistently aware of your account metrics allows you to make informed decisions quickly, avoiding unnecessary surprises.

A tip from seasoned traders: focus not just on potential returns but on potential risks as well. Examine worst-case scenarios for every trade you place. What happens if the market moves X% against you? Can your margin cover that? By simulating these scenarios, you prepare mentally and financially for adverse market conditions, enhancing your ability to react calmly and decisively.

Lastly, never shy away from seeking advice and learning from experienced traders. Mentorship can provide valuable insights tailored to your specific trading style and goals. Many pros will stress the importance of managing leverage and margin, reinforcing that it's not just about how much you can gain, but how well you can protect what you have.

Managing leverage and margin is an ongoing process. It requires vigilance, discipline, and a bit of humility to understand that markets can be unpredictable. By familiarizing yourself with these concepts and integrating them into your broader risk management strategy, you'll stand a much better chance of navigating the Forex market successfully. So, keep learning, stay disciplined, and always trade with a clear understanding of how leverage and margin impact your positions. It's this balanced approach that will pave the way for your long-term success in the Forex market.

The 1% Risk Rule

The 1% Risk Rule is a cornerstone of sound risk management in Forex trading, often heralded as the golden standard among both novice and seasoned traders. This rule suggests that you should never risk more than 1% of your trading account on a single trade. Simple yet effective, it is designed to protect your capital and keep you in the game, even during losing streaks. Implementing the 1% Risk Rule can mean the difference between surviving a volatile market and facing the dreaded margin call.

So, why 1%? It's a number that strikes a balance between taking meaningful risks and safeguarding your trading account from significant losses. If you have a trading account worth $10,000, for example, using the 1% Risk Rule means you would not risk more than $100 on any single trade. This conservative approach may seem overly cautious to some, but its virtue lies in sustainability. By limiting your risk to 1% of your capital, you ensure that a few bad trades won't wipe out your account, giving you more opportunities to succeed in the long run.

Adherence to the 1% Risk Rule requires discipline. It's easy to become overconfident after a string of successful trades and double down on your next position. However, this greed-driven behavior often leads to substantial losses. The rule forces you to approach each trade with the same degree of caution, minimizing emotional decision-making which can be detrimental to your trading performance. Remember, surviving in Forex trading is not just about making winning trades but managing losing ones effectively.

Let's delve into a practical example. Say you're eyeing a promising trade on the EUR/USD pair and you've determined that a reasonable stop loss for this trade would be 50 pips. With the 1% Risk Rule in mind and a trading account of $10,000, you would calculate your position size as follows: since you're willing to risk $100 and your stop loss is 50 pips, each pip should represent $2. Therefore, your position size would be 0.02 lots. This example, though straightforward, encapsulates the necessity of integrating risk and position sizing into your trading plan.

By following this rule, you're also aligning your trading behavior with the mathematical realities of probabilistic outcomes. No matter how skilled or knowledgeable you are, some trades will inevitably be losers. The 1% Risk Rule mitigates the impact of these losses, allowing for longer survivability and thus greater chances of profiting over time. Statistically, the key is to let your winning trades outnumber and outweigh your losing ones, a goal more achievable when you're not taking massive hits to your account balance.

The psychological benefits of the 1% Risk Rule are equally compelling. Knowing that you are only risking a small fraction of your account on any single trade helps alleviate anxiety and fosters a more relaxed trading mindset. You're less likely to panic during temporary price fluctuations or make rash decisions. This mental calmness allows for more objective market analysis and better decision-making, which are critical for long-term trading success.

The 1% Risk Rule also dovetails perfectly with other risk management techniques like setting stop-loss orders and managing leverage. When you apply the 1% rule, your stop-loss levels become more meaningful, serving as well-calculated safety nets rather than arbitrary limits. Additionally, it curbs the temptation to over-leverage. In Forex trading, leverage can amplify both gains and losses, and misusing it can devastate your account. The 1% rule ensures that even with higher leverage, the actual risk remains controlled.

Despite its advantages, some critics argue that the 1% Risk Rule is too restrictive and reduces the potential for substantial gains. However, the aim isn't to seek short-term profits but to build a stable and profitable trading career over the long haul. Traders who risk large portions of their accounts can indeed see big wins, but they are just as likely to experience devastating losses. The 1% Rule may seem conservative, but it's a small price to pay for lasting in an arena rife with volatility.

Moreover, this rule isn't set in stone. Depending on your risk tolerance and experience level, you might opt for a slightly higher percentage, such as 2%, particularly if you have proven, consistent trading success over time. However, novices should stick strictly to the 1% Rule until they have amassed enough experience and a solid track record of disciplined trading. Adjustments can be made as your expertise grows and as you refine your risk management strategies.

To effectively implement the 1% Risk Rule, it's crucial to include it as an integral part of your trading plan. From your first trade, consistency is key. Regularly revisit and review your trading plan to ensure you are adhering to this rule. Making exceptions or bending it for seemingly "sure bets" can quickly turn into a slippery slope toward reckless trading behavior.

Another practical tip: use trading journals to keep track of how well you adhere to the 1% Risk Rule. By logging each trade, you can analyze whether you've adhered to your risk management principles or deviated. Through this self-reflection, you'll gain insights into your trading habits and areas for improvement. It's a practice that ties into the broader theme of continual learning and improvement, which is vital for long-term success in Forex trading.

The 1% Risk Rule is more than just a guideline; it's a mindset, a discipline, and a commitment to the principles of prudent trading. It encourages patience and an analytical approach, steering you away from the harmful impulsiveness that often plagues traders. By consistently applying this rule, you're laying a foundation for sustainable success, ensuring that your trading journey is marked by steady growth and risk-controlled progress.

Remember, the key to mastery in Forex trading is not in the sheer number of successful trades but in the effective management of your entire trading portfolio. The 1% Risk Rule stands as a testament to this principle, advocating for a cautious but calculated approach to every trade you undertake. Through its application, you'll not only safeguard your hard-earned capital but also build a disciplined and resilient trading strategy that can weather the highs and lows of the Forex market.

CHAPTER 8:
MAKING THE TRADE

S tepping into the realm of live trading, it's crucial to grasp the mechanics of placing a trade seamlessly. Key to this is understanding order types and execution methods, ensuring you're not just winging it but executing trades with precision. Trading sessions and timing play an equally pivotal role; knowing the best times to trade can be the difference between riding a trend and getting caught in a whipsaw. Each trading session—be it Tokyo, London, or New York—holds its distinct characteristics, influencing volatility and liquidity. By mastering these elements, you fortify your trading strategy with informed decisions, enhancing your ability to navigate the dynamic Forex market with confidence and agility.

The Mechanics of Placing a Trade

The Mechanics of Placing a Trade embody the fundamental process central to Forex trading success. Understanding the step-by-step procedures ensures you navigate the market with clarity and confidence. Whether you're executing a simple buy or sell order or employing more complex strategies, the mechanics remain consistent. Let's break down this process in detail so you can place your trades efficiently.

First, you must decide on the currency pair you wish to trade. Each pair consists of a base currency and a quote currency. For example, in the EUR/USD pair, the euro (EUR) is the base currency, and the US dollar (USD) is the quote currency. Your goal is to trade one currency for another, predicting the movement in the exchange rate. If you expect the base currency to appreciate

74

against the quote currency, you will place a buy order. Conversely, if you anticipate depreciation, you will place a sell order.

Next, determine the entry point for your trade. This decision might rely on your analysis—either through fundamental or technical strategies. Timing your entry can be crucial; enter too early, and the market might move against you, but enter too late, and you could miss out on profits. Many traders set specific criteria for their entries to minimize guesswork, such as waiting for certain technical indicators to align or for fundamental news to break.

Once you've decided on your entry point, logging into your trading platform is the next step. Ensure you're familiar with the functionalities and tools available. Platforms like MetaTrader 4 and 5, cTrader, and various broker-proprietary platforms offer different features to aid your trading experience. Take some time to understand how to navigate and place orders before risking any real capital.

Before executing your trade, you must decide on the trade size. This factor is often expressed in 'lots.' In Forex, there are three common lot sizes: standard, mini, and micro. A standard lot equals 100,000 units of the base currency, a mini lot equals 10,000 units, and a micro lot equals 1,000 units. Novice traders often start with mini or micro lots to manage risk better, as trading standard lots can lead to significant gains or losses quickly.

Now, place your trade. Open the trading platform and select the currency pair you're interested in. Choose whether you're buying or selling and specify the trade size. You'll also need to set the appropriate order type, such as a market order, limit order, or stop order. A market order buys or sells immediately at the current market price, while a limit order buys or sells at a specific price in the future. Stop orders execute once a particular price is reached, resembling a combination of automatic and conditional execution.

It's not enough to place a trade; you need to manage it actively. Set your stop loss and take profit levels to protect your capital and lock in gains. A stop loss order automatically closes your trade at a predetermined price to limit losses. Conversely, a take profit order sets a price to close your trade, securing profits once your target is reached. Utilizing these tools can instill discipline and help you adhere to your risk management strategy.

After placing your trade and setting up protective measures, monitoring your position is essential. Markets are dynamic and can change rapidly due to various factors: economic data releases, geopolitical events, or unexpected global incidents. Regularly reviewing your trades ensures you can adjust stop-loss and take-profit levels or even close trades early to mitigate losses or secure profits.

Beyond the basics, the mechanics of placing a trade also involve continuously learning and adapting. As you gain more trading experience, you'll develop a deeper understanding of how market forces interact and how specific news events might affect your trades. Keeping a trading journal, as discussed in a later chapter, can be invaluable for recording your decisions and their outcomes, allowing for periodic reviews and strategy refinements.

Moreover, practicing placing trades in a demo account can be invaluable for those just starting. Demo accounts provide a risk-free environment to test and refine your trading skills. They replicate the trading platform experience but with virtual funds instead of real capital. This practice can build your confidence and help you better understand the intricacies of the trade placement process without financial risk.

Finally, consider leveraging the resources at your disposal. Various online tutorials, webinars, and broker-provided educational materials can offer further insight into the mechanics of placing a trade. Joining communities or forums can also provide practical tips and support from more experienced traders, enriching your knowledge base and strategy toolkit.

Effectively grasping these mechanics equips you to make well-informed and strategic decisions in the Forex market. As you continue to trade, these actions will become more intuitive, allowing you to focus on analyzing the market and refining your trading strategies rather than being bogged down by technicalities.

Mastery of the mechanics is a pivotal step towards becoming a proficient and confident Forex trader.

Order Types and Execution

Order Types and Execution serve as fundamental concepts in mastering Forex trading. To make informed and effective decisions, understanding the different types of orders and how they are executed is crucial. Whether you are a novice or a seasoned trader, mastering these elements can significantly influence your trading success.

At its core, an order represents a trader's instructions to either buy or sell a certain amount of a currency pair. You make these orders through your broker, who then facilitates the transaction in the Forex market. There are several types of orders, each designed to meet specific trading objectives and risk management strategies. Let's explore the most important ones.

A market order is the most straightforward type. With this order, you instruct your broker to buy or sell a currency pair immediately at the current market price. This type of order guarantees execution and is typically used when entering or exiting a position swiftly. However, one downside is potential slippage, where the executed price differs slightly from the expected price due to rapid market movements.

Limit orders, on the other hand, give you more control over the execution price. If you place a limit order to buy, you specify the maximum price you are willing to pay. Conversely, a limit order to sell specifies the minimum price you are willing to accept. These orders are executed only when the market reaches your set price or better. While they help in achieving a more favorable price, there is a risk that the market never reaches your specified price, resulting in a missed opportunity.

Stop orders serve another vital purpose in trading. A stop order activates a market order once a specified price level is reached. Often used as a risk management tool, a stop-loss order can help you limit your losses. For instance, setting a stop-loss ensures that if the market moves against your position, your trade will automatically close at a predefined price level, reducing the potential for substantial losses.

Then we have stop-limit orders, which combine elements of both stop and limit orders. Here, when the specified stop price is reached, the order converts into a limit order instead of a market order. While this gives you more control over the execution, there's a notable risk: in volatile markets, your limit price may never be met, leaving your position open longer than anticipated.

Another less common but useful order type is the trailing stop order. This dynamic risk management tool allows your stop price to adjust as the market price moves in your favor. Essentially, it "trails" the market price by a specified distance. If the market reverses, the trailing stop can help lock in profits by triggering a sell order at the new level.

The functionality of these orders depends largely on the execution process. For example, the speed and efficiency with which your broker handles your orders can have a substantial impact. Some brokers offer different execution models, such as "instant execution" and "market execution," that can influence how your orders are filled.

Instant execution occurs when your order is executed at the price you see on your trading platform. This can be beneficial in stable markets but may result in rejected orders during highly volatile periods. On the flip side, market execution means your order is filled at the best available price at that moment, which could vary slightly from the price displayed on your screen.

Understanding the different types of execution models can help you choose a broker that aligns with your trading style. Additionally, it's essential to be aware of potential issues like requotes, slippage, and latency, each of which can affect the final outcome of your trades.

Now let's discuss how these order types fit into your overall trading strategy. Utilizing a mix of market, limit, and stop orders can offer a balance between achieving favorable prices and managing risk. For example, you might use a limit order to enter a trade at a desirable price point, along with a stop-loss order to mitigate potential losses.

Also, the type of order you choose may depend on the trading session. Forex operates 24 hours a day, but not all hours are created equal. Liquidity and volatility vary significantly during different sessions, such as the Tokyo, London, and New York sessions. Placing orders during high liquidity periods can help ensure better execution and lower the risk of slippage.

In practice, setting up these orders requires familiarity with your trading platform. Most platforms allow you to configure orders easily, providing various options for tailoring the execution to meet your needs. Take time to understand the specific features and options offered by your platform to make the most of your trading.

Over time, as you gain experience, you'll become more adept at choosing the right types of orders for different market conditions. Continually evaluate your strategies and make adjustments based on your evolving understanding of order types and market dynamics.

Finally, remember that no single order type or execution model fits all trading scenarios. Flexibility and adaptability are key to successful trading. Be prepared to adjust your approach as market conditions change and as you gain more experience.

In summary, grasping the nuances of order types and execution can greatly elevate your trading effectiveness. While this knowledge forms a foundation, the practical application and continual refinement of these concepts in real-world trading scenarios will truly empower you to navigate the Forex market with assurance and skill.

Trading Sessions and Best Times to Trade

Trading Sessions and Best Times to Trade are critical aspects every budding Forex trader needs to grasp. Each trading session offers unique characteristics, volatility levels, and market behavior, shaping the way traders strategize and execute their trades.

The Forex market operates 24 hours a day, five days a week, because it spans across various global financial centers. The key trading sessions are the Sydney, Tokyo, London, and New York sessions. These sessions don't all operate in isolation—there are overlaps between them which create some of the most opportune times to trade.

The **first session** to kick things off is the Sydney session, which opens at 10 PM GMT and closes at 7 AM GMT. Though it's a relatively smaller market, it's crucial for traders interested in the Australian dollar because Australian economic data is often released during this time. This session might be quieter compared to others but offers steady trends which could benefit traders looking for less volatile conditions.

The **Tokyo session** opens right after Sydney at 12 AM GMT and closes at 9 AM GMT. Forex traders will notice increased liquidity during this session, especially in currency pairs involving the Japanese yen. Tokyo is a significant financial hub, and economic data from Japan can greatly influence market movements. The Tokyo session also overlaps with the end of the Sydney session, creating a period of higher activity. Many traders focus on breakout strategies during this session due to the volatility brought about by economic news releases.

The real pace begins with the **London session**, the largest and most active trading session. It starts at 8 AM GMT and closes at 5 PM GMT. London's market accounts for a significant portion of daily Forex trading volume. The session is renowned for its sharp price movements and high liquidity, making it ideal for nearly any type of trading strategy. Trades during this period often involve the euro, pound, and Swiss franc. Due to the high trading volume, trends are often clearer, giving traders the potential to latch onto longer-lasting moves. When the London session overlaps with the end of the Tokyo session, typically the hour around 8 AM GMT to 9 AM GMT, it's particularly vibrant and filled with opportunities.

The final session in the trading day is the **New York session**, which opens at 1 PM GMT and closes at 10 PM GMT. As the second-largest Forex trading market, New York adds substantial volume and volatility into the mix. Key economic data releases from the United States, such as the Non-Farm Payrolls, impact currency movements significantly. The first few hours of the New York session are especially noteworthy as they overlap with the later half of the London session. This overlap creates one of the most anticipated times in Forex trading, with price fluctuations providing high-profit potential.

For optimal trading, understanding these overlaps is crucial. The periods when two sessions overlap typically see increased trading activity and liquidity. The main overlaps are:

- **Tokyo and London overlap**: 8 AM GMT to 9 AM GMT

- **London and New York overlap**: 1 PM GMT to 5 PM GMT

During these overlaps, the market witnesses some of the highest trading volumes, leading to more defined trends and reduced spreads. These conditions are ideal for both short-term traders looking for quick gains and long-term traders interested in catching the day's primary trend.

While the technical aspects are critical, there's also a psychological edge to trading during these sessions. Being able to focus your trading activities during peak times means you can avoid periods of inactivity and low volatility, which often lead to trading errors and diminished focus. Trading at the right times helps not just in achieving better execution but also in maintaining a disciplined trading routine.

It's essential to align your trading activities to your personal schedule as well. Suppose you reside in a time zone that doesn't comfortably align with the more active sessions. In that case, you might consider focusing on the crossover periods or adapt your strategies to the quieter periods. Additionally, even though Forex trading can be exciting, taking breaks and not overtrading is just as crucial to long-term success. Remember, the best trades often come from the best-planned and well-timed entries.

To leverage these trading sessions effectively, it's vital to stay informed about economic news and events. Utilize an *economic calendar* to keep track of data releases that could affect currency pairs you're trading. Announcements during or just before the start of each session can set the tone for the day's price direction. Planning your trades around these releases can give you an added advantage.

Furthermore, each currency pair has its own peak time coinciding with the time zone of the pair's currency countries. For instance, EUR/USD will be most active during the London session and early New York session, while AUD/JPY will see higher activity during the Sydney and Tokyo sessions.

Lastly, practicing good risk management is non-negotiable. High activity periods can generate larger profits but also come with increased risk. Use stop-loss orders and set realistic profit targets to safeguard your investment. Making educated, well-timed trades is at the heart of successful Forex trading.

So, knowing the dynamics of the **trading sessions and the best times to trade** is non-negotiable. Mastering the unique characteristics of each session, and understanding the interplay between them can significantly enhance your trading performance. By aligning your strategies to these sessions and overlaps, you position yourself to capitalize on the market's most lucrative hours while managing your risk effectively.

CHAPTER 9:
ADVANCED TRADING CONCEPTS

D iving into advanced trading concepts, we're moving beyond the basics to explore strategies and techniques that can significantly enhance your trading prowess. In this chapter, you'll discover how to use Fibonacci retracement levels to predict potential market reversals and identify profitable entry and exit points. We'll delve into the concept of divergence, helping you understand how discrepancies between price movement and indicators can signal potential trend changes. Additionally, we'll analyze currency correlations, giving you insights into how different currency pairs move in relation to one another and how this can affect your trading decisions. Mastering these advanced concepts won't just refine your existing skills but will also equip you with a deeper understanding of market dynamics, setting the stage for more nuanced and successful trading decisions.

Using Fibonacci in Forex

Using Fibonacci in Forex is an advanced trading technique rooted in a sequence of numbers first identified by the Italian mathematician Leonardo Fibonacci in the 13th century. This method has become a staple in the toolkit of many forex traders due to its ability to predict potential price retracement levels. In this section, we'll delve into how to effectively use Fibonacci retracement and extension levels to enhance your trading strategy.

At the core of Fibonacci analysis in forex trading is the Fibonacci sequence, where each number is the sum of the two preceding ones: 0, 1, 1, 2, 3, 5, 8, 13, and so on. This sequence translates into percentage ratios often used in trading – specifically,

23.6%, 38.2%, 50%, 61.8%, and 100%. Traders use these ratios to identify key levels where price might experience support or resistance.

Let's start with Fibonacci retracements. These are used to determine how far the market has moved against its recent direction. To plot a Fibonacci retracement on a forex chart, identify a significant peak and trough. For example, if a currency pair has moved from 1.2000 to 1.3000, the Fibonacci retracement levels will be calculated based on that 1000-pip range. Draw the retracement grid from the bottom to the top of this move. The levels you've indicated – 23.6%, 38.2%, 50%, and 61.8% – become potential areas of support (if the market is bullish) or resistance (if the market is bearish) where the price may pause or reverse.

What makes Fibonacci retracement levels compelling is their self-fulfilling nature. Many traders watch these levels closely, which often results in a significant amount of buying or selling interest around them. For instance, a retracement to the 50% level might coincide with other technical factors such as historical support, leading to a higher probability that the price will bounce up from this point.

On the other hand, Fibonacci extensions are used to predict where the price will go next after retracement levels have been broken. Extensions include levels like 161.8%, 261.8%, and 423.6%. Plotting extensions follows a similar process but with a focus on forecasting future price action. If a currency pair retraces from a downward move and then continues to rise, Fibonacci extensions can help determine where the price might encounter future resistance.

For practical illustration, suppose you're trading the EUR/USD pair, which has risen from 1.1000 to 1.1500. After reaching this recent high, the pair starts to dip. You plot Fibonacci retracement levels on this upward movement. As the price retraces, you notice hesitation around the 38.2% retracement level of 1.1300. This could signal a potential buying opportunity if other indicators, such as volume and candlestick patterns, also suggest a bullish reversal.

It's essential to integrate Fibonacci tools with other technical indicators to improve their reliability. For example, combining Fibonacci retracement levels with trend lines or moving averages can significantly enhance your analysis. If a retracement level coincides with a long-term moving average, the chances of that level holding as support or resistance increase dramatically.

Another critical pattern to recognize when using Fibonacci tools is confluence. Confluence occurs when different technical factors align at the same price level. Suppose a key Fibonacci retracement aligns with a historical support level and a psychological round number. This triple confluence can make the level even more powerful, increasing the likelihood of a strong price reaction.

Despite their utility, Fibonacci techniques aren't foolproof. They're best used as part of a broader trading strategy that includes risk management principles. Remember to set stop-loss orders to protect your capital if the market moves against you. Additionally, practice using Fibonacci tools on a demo account to gain confidence and refine your skills before applying them in a live trading environment.

Moreover, understanding the context and market conditions during which Fibonacci levels are applied is crucial. In trending markets, Fibonacci retracement levels can offer excellent entry points for trading with the trend. In contrast, during sideways markets, these levels may be less reliable as the price action lacks a clear directional bias.

Take time to backtest your strategies with historical data to see how effectively Fibonacci levels predicted retracement and extension points. While past performance doesn't guarantee future results, backtesting can provide invaluable insights and help tweak your approach to different market scenarios.

To summarize, using Fibonacci in forex trading involves identifying potential points of support and resistance by plotting retracement and extension levels based on recent price movements. While these techniques are not infallible, they can be powerful tools when used in conjunction with other analysis methods and a robust risk management plan. By mastering Fibonacci analysis, you can add a significant edge to your forex trading arsenal, helping you make more informed decisions and increasing your chances of success in the fast-paced world of currency trading.

The Role of Divergence

The Role of Divergence is an intriguing concept in the realm of Forex trading, offering traders invaluable insights into potential market movements. Divergence occurs when the price of a currency pair and an indicator, such as the Relative Strength Index (RSI) or Moving Average Convergence Divergence (MACD), move in opposite directions. It signals that the current trend may be weakening, potentially leading to a reversal or significant correction. Understanding and identifying divergence can give traders an edge by alerting them to shifts in market sentiment before the broader market catches on.

Divergence can be categorized mainly into two types: regular divergence and hidden divergence. Regular divergence provides early signals of trend reversals and occurs when the price forms higher highs while the indicator forms lower highs, or vice versa for downward trends. Hidden divergence, on the other hand, is seen as a continuation signal, indicating that a trend is likely to continue. It happens when the price forms lower highs during an uptrend or higher lows during a downtrend, while the indicator shows the opposite.

Let's delve deeper into regular divergence. Consider it a red flag alerting you to potential turning points. For instance, if the price of a currency pair is making higher highs but the RSI is making lower highs, it might be time to prepare for a decline. This inconsistency suggests the buying pressure is diminishing, and the current upward trend might soon reverse. By recognizing these cues, you can either exit your position to safeguard profits or take a counter-trend position to capitalize on the anticipated market shift.

Hidden divergence, though less dramatic, is equally powerful. It reinforces the strength of an existing trend. When you see hidden divergence, such as a series of higher lows in price but lower lows in the indicator during an uptrend, it indicates that the market still has the momentum to maintain its direction. Traders often use this signal to add to their existing positions or as a confirmation to hold onto their trades, expecting the trend to persist.

For effective utilization of divergence in your trading strategy, combining it with other technical analysis tools is crucial. Solely relying on divergence can lead to false signals and potential losses. When you pair divergence with trend lines, support and resistance levels, or candlestick patterns, you add layers of confirmation that can greatly increase your trading accuracy. For instance, if divergence aligns with a major support level and a bullish candlestick pattern, it strengthens the case for a buy signal.

To illustrate, imagine you're examining the EUR/USD pair. You've identified a potential uptrend, and you spot regular bearish divergence; the price is climbing, but the MACD histogram is getting shorter. Simultaneously, you discern that the upward movement is approaching a well-established resistance zone. All these signals combined provide a compelling reason to anticipate a price reversal. By integrating these multiple layers of analysis, your trading decisions will be more informed and robust.

Backtesting plays a crucial role in mastering the application of divergence in your trading. By reviewing historical data and simulating trades based on divergence signals, you can gauge the effectiveness and refine your approach. This practice not only boosts your confidence but also helps you develop an eye for recognizing genuine signals versus noise. Remember, the goal is to discern clear, actionable patterns amidst the market's inherent volatility.

In addition to backtesting, real-time practice in a demo trading environment can be incredibly beneficial. It offers you the chance to apply your divergence-based strategies without financial risk, further solidifying your understanding and skillset. By experimenting with different currency pairs and time frames, you'll gain a comprehensive perspective on how divergence behaves across various market conditions.

A key aspect worth noting is emotional discipline. Divergence signals, like any other trading indicator, are not infallible. Occasionally, they might mislead, tempting you to act impulsively. It's essential to stay calm, adhere to your trading plan, and not overreact to a single signal. Consistency and patience often triumph over knee-jerk reactions in the long run.

Further enhancing your divergence technique involves staying informed about market-moving events. Economic indicators, geopolitical developments, and central bank policies can all impact currency movements, sometimes rendering technical signals less reliable. By keeping an ear to the ground and integrating fundamental analysis with your technical approach, you can navigate Forex markets with a holistic perspective.

In sum, **The Role of Divergence** serves as a significant analytical tool in Forex trading, offering predictive insights into market trends. Whether signaling potential reversals with regular divergence or trend continuations with hidden divergence, it equips traders with an additional layer of market analysis. When used in conjunction with other technical tools and solid risk management practices, divergence can enhance your trading strategy, contributing to more informed decision-making and ultimately, trading success.

Understanding Currency Correlations

Understanding Currency Correlations is vital for anyone serious about navigating the Forex market. Put simply, currency correlations measure how two different currency pairs move in relation to each other. This relationship can be positive or negative.

Positive correlation means that as one currency pair rises, the other is likely to rise too, and vice versa. Negative correlation implies that when one pair goes up, the other typically goes down. Understanding these dynamics can significantly enhance your trading strategies and risk management.

Imagine you're monitoring two currency pairs: EUR/USD and GBP/USD. A positive correlation between these pairs indicates that they usually move in sync. This correlation might arise because both pairs share the US dollar as a common currency. Conversely, a pair like USD/JPY might have a negative correlation with EUR/USD, meaning if the EUR/USD goes up, the USD/JPY generally heads down. Recognizing such patterns allows traders to make more informed decisions and manage risk better.

Why do these correlations exist? Several factors contribute, including economic ties, political situations, and monetary policies among the involved countries. For instance, the economies of the Eurozone and the United Kingdom are closely linked. Therefore, the EUR/USD and GBP/USD pairs often move in tandem. Conversely, a currency pair like the USD/JPY may react differently to global events compared to the EUR/USD because of differing economic policies and geopolitical factors.

Understanding currency correlations also helps diversify your portfolio. By knowing which pairs move together and which move inversely, you can strategically place trades to balance your risk. For instance, if you're long on EUR/USD and long on GBP/USD, you're essentially doubling down on the USD weakening. However, if you combine long on EUR/USD with short on USD/JPY, you're diversifying your risk because these pairs often move inversely.

A useful tool to quantify these relationships is the correlation coefficient—a statistical measure ranging from +1 to -1. A coefficient closer to +1 means the pairs have a strong positive correlation, while one nearing -1 indicates a strong negative correlation. A coefficient around zero implies no meaningful relationship between the pairs. Most trading platforms provide these figures, making it easier to plan your trades.

Monitoring these correlations can also warn you when something unusual is happening. Suppose the correlation between two normally positively correlated pairs suddenly becomes negative. This shift could be a signal to dig deeper into the underlying causes—whether it's a political upheaval, economic data release, or a sudden market sentiment change. Such awareness can prevent you from making poorly informed trading decisions.

Currency correlations aren't static; they evolve. Economic conditions, changes in government, or even shifts in market sentiment can alter how currency pairs interact. Regularly updating yourself on these correlations can provide a more accurate and current trading strategy. Tools and resources are available that offer real-time correlation data, incorporating these into your routine can enhance your forex trading journey.

For instance, if a central bank like the Fed decides to change interest rates, the USD might strengthen or weaken broadly, affecting multiple currency pairs differently. Staying attuned to such macroeconomic changes ensures that your understanding of currency correlations isn't outdated. Regular reading of financial news, economic forecasts, and trading forums can keep your correlations knowledge as accurate as possible.

In addition to enhancing your trading strategies, understanding currency correlations can also prevent redundant trades. Let's say you decide to open multiple positions thinking you're diversifying, but if those currency pairs are positively correlated, you're not spreading your risk effectively. Instead, evaluating the correlations can guide you to make trades that genuinely balance your risk exposure.

Moreover, knowing about correlations allows you to better calculate your risk. When you open trades in multiple pairs, considering their correlations can give you a more accurate picture of your overall risk. For example, if you're highly leveraged on positively correlated pairs, a negative move could amplify losses across all those trades. Conversely, understanding these relationships can mitigate such risks.

Another practical use of currency correlations is during times of market uncertainty. Suppose a geopolitical event impacts the market, understanding how different pairs might react can offer trading opportunities. For example, if a political crisis hits the Eurozone, not only would the EUR/USD likely plummet, but correlated pairs like EUR/GBP might also see significant movement. Being prepared for such scenarios is crucial for effective risk management. Savvy traders use these correlations to hedge against potential losses by taking positions in negatively correlated pairs.

It's also worth mentioning that tools and calculators are available to aid traders in understanding these correlations. Several online platforms offer real-time correlation matrices that show how various currency pairs relate to each other. Utilizing these tools can simplify your trading process, making it easier to balance your portfolio and manage risk. Some brokers even provide built-in correlation tools within their trading platforms, offering on-the-go analysis.

To wrap it all up, mastering currency correlations can dramatically improve your Forex trading skills. By understanding how different pairs interact, you can construct more robust trading strategies and better manage your risks. While this requires continuous learning and adjustment as market conditions change, the payoff in trading efficiency and profitability is well worth the effort.

CHAPTER 10:
KEEPING A TRADING JOURNAL

Keeping a trading journal is a pivotal step in honing your Forex trading skills. It's more than just a diary; it's a powerful tool for self-reflection and continuous improvement. In your journal, you'll note down not only the specifics of each trade, such as entry and exit points, but also the underlying rationale, emotional state, and any unforeseen events that influenced your decisions. By regularly reviewing your journal, you can identify patterns, recognize your strengths, and pinpoint areas that need work. This practice fosters a disciplined trading mindset and allows you to adapt and optimize your strategy over time, making you a more confident and skilled trader.

Benefits of a Trading Journal

Benefits of a Trading Journal Imagine venturing into the world of currency trading without a map or a log to track your journey. It'd be chaotic. That's where a trading journal comes in. Think of it as your personal guide—a place where you document your trades, strategies, successes, and yes, even your mistakes. The benefits of maintaining a trading journal are profound, especially when you're new to Forex trading.

A trading journal acts as a reflective tool, enabling you to learn from your past actions. By meticulously recording each trade, you can uncover patterns in your trading behavior that you might not notice otherwise. For instance, you might realize that you're consistently more successful when trading during certain market conditions or that specific currency pairs yield better results. This self-awareness is crucial for honing your skills and enhancing your trading strategy.

Another significant benefit is the ability to track your progress over time. When you're embroiled in the day-to-day fluctuations of the Forex market, it can be challenging to see the bigger picture. A well-maintained journal allows you to step back and see how far you've come. Imagine flipping through pages of recorded trades and realizing that you've gradually improved your win rate or successfully limited your losses. It's a motivational boost that keeps you aligned with your long-term goals.

The discipline required to maintain a trading journal can't be overstated. The act of writing down every trade reinforces a mindset of accountability. You're less likely to make impulsive, emotionally-driven decisions when you know you'll have to honestly record and analyze them later. This habit cultivates a disciplined approach, encouraging you to follow your trading plan and adhere to your risk management rules rigorously.

Your trading journal isn't just about numbers and transactions. It's also a space for introspection, where you can jot down your emotional state and thoughts during each trade. Did a certain trade make you anxious? Were you overconfident after a winning streak? Identifying emotional triggers helps you manage psychological pitfalls like fear and greed—common adversaries in the Forex market. In essence, your journal becomes a mirror reflecting both your technical and emotional journey.

Furthermore, a detailed trading journal serves as an excellent educational resource. Reviewing your records allows you to analyze the effectiveness of various strategies you've deployed. Here's where you identify what's working and what's not. Suppose you've tried using different indicators or experimented with various entry and exit points. By comparing these variables against your trading outcomes, you can refine your approach and optimize your strategies over time.

One of the more understated advantages of a trading journal is that it can significantly enhance your risk management. By keeping track of your trades, you can identify how well you stick to your risk management rules, such as stop-loss and take-profit levels. Over time, you'll be able to see if you're consistently risking too much on trades or if you're frequently moving your stop-loss orders after entering a trade. This level of scrutiny ensures that you stay vigilant about managing your risk, which is fundamental for long-term success in Forex trading.

You'll find that maintaining a trading journal also strengthens your analytical skills. As you regularly analyze your trades, you become more adept at recognizing market trends, spotting potential opportunities, and avoiding common pitfalls. This improved analytical ability is invaluable when navigating the complexities of the Forex market. The skills you develop here are transferable, meaning they'll serve you well in other areas of trading or even in different financial markets.

A trading journal is not just for solitary benefits; it can be a valuable tool when seeking mentorship. Sharing your detailed trading journal with a mentor provides them with the insights they need to give targeted advice. Your mentor will be able to pinpoint areas of strength and weakness and offer actionable recommendations based on your documented trading history. Such tailored guidance can accelerate your learning curve and significantly improve your trading performance.

In situations where you need to evaluate the effectiveness of new trading strategies or tools, your journal becomes your testing ground. When you record the results of these new strategies, you can objectively compare them against your existing methods to see which provides better returns or complements your trading style. This way, your journal serves as a controlled environment for experimentation, reducing the risk of making significant changes based on untested methods.

Additionally, in the ever-evolving landscape of Forex trading, staying adaptable is crucial. A trading journal helps you adapt by providing a clear record of how various market conditions, news events, or geopolitical developments impact your trades. This historical data allows you to develop flexible strategies that can be adjusted as market conditions change. Instead of reacting impulsively to market movements, you'll be making informed decisions backed by your thorough records.

Finally, let's not underestimate the psychological comfort a trading journal offers. The Forex market can be overwhelming, especially for beginners. Having a structured approach and a log of all your trades can give you a sense of control and reduce anxiety. Knowing that you have a reliable method for tracking and analyzing your progress provides peace of mind, enabling you to focus on improving your trading skills rather than worrying about every market fluctuation.

In essence, the benefits of a trading journal go beyond mere record-keeping. It's a comprehensive tool that fosters discipline, enhances analytical skills, supports emotional stability, and enables strategic refinement. For anyone serious about thriving in the Forex market, a trading journal is indispensable, guiding you towards informed decisions and sustained success. By committing to detailed and diligent journaling, you're setting the foundation for a rewarding journey in currency trading.

What to Record in Your

What to Record in Your Journal plays a critical role in your growth as a Forex trader. It serves as an indispensable tool for monitoring your progress, understanding your trading patterns, and refining your strategies. The essence of journaling in Forex trading is not merely to document your trades but to provide an insightful analysis of your actions, decisions, and the market conditions. This practice not only sharpens your decision-making skills but also propels you towards becoming a more disciplined and effective trader.

Start each journal entry with the basics: the date and time of the trade, the currency pair traded, and the type of order executed. Recording this fundamental information ensures you have precise timelines and can track your activity over specific periods. It also allows you to later analyze which trading sessions work best for you and which currency pairs yield the most consistent results. Furthermore, noting the type of order helps in understanding how different order types align with your trading strategy.

Dive deeper by documenting the reasoning behind each trade. This includes jotting down the technical indicators and fundamental factors that influenced your decision. For instance, if you entered a trade based on a support level, write down which chart patterns you observed and why you believed the price would bounce back. If economic news drove the trade, specify what news event occurred and how you expected it to impact the currency pair. By doing this, you give yourself a chance to scrutinize your decision-making process, helping you separate instinct from calculated analysis.

It's equally important to make a note of your emotions before, during, and after the trade. Acknowledge if you felt confident, anxious, or uncertain. Emotional factors often cloud judgements and hinder the efficacy of even the most robust trading strategies. Recording your emotional state can unveil patterns that indicate when you might be trading on impulse or emotion rather than a logical strategy. This self-awareness is crucial for developing emotional discipline and avoiding the pitfalls of fear and greed.

Your journal should also include the specifics of your risk management measures—like the stop loss and take profit levels you set for each trade. Analyzing these elements over time reveals whether your risk management strategies are effective or need adjustment. Tracking these figures can also highlight if you're consistently risking too much on trades, offering an opportunity to realign with principles such as the 1% Risk Rule covered in Chapter 7.

Additionally, record the outcome of each trade in detail. Did you hit your target or stop loss? Was there slippage? How did the market behave post-entry and exit? This data is invaluable for backtesting and refining your strategy. It allows you to learn from both your successes and failures, providing concrete evidence on which approaches yield results and which don't.

To get a full grasp on the efficacy of your trading strategy, keep a periodic summary of your performance. This could be weekly, monthly, or quarterly, depending on how frequently you trade. Summarize the number of trades executed, the win-loss ratio, average return on investment, and the total gains or losses. Consolidating this data over regular intervals helps you gauge your overall performance and make informed decisions about whether to stick with or modify your current strategy.

Beyond the metrics and technicalities, jot down any peculiarities or anomalies you notice. Was there an unexpected market move? Did a specific indicator fail to perform as anticipated? Did you observe any news event surprisingly affecting a currency pair? These intricate details can sometimes shed light on trends or market behaviors that can be valuable in future trades.

Your trading journal can also benefit from including insights and recommendations. After analyzing a trade, write down what you think went well and what could have been done differently. Propose adjustments to your trading plan or strategies based on these observations. These insights serve as a living document of your journey, constantly evolving as you learn and grow in your trading experience.

Lastly, don't overlook the importance of reviewing your journal regularly. This practice helps reinforce lessons learned and avoids repeating past mistakes. Set aside dedicated time for these reviews, just as you would for market analysis. Regularly examining your journal keeps you aligned with your goals and committed to continual improvement.

The act of maintaining and revisiting a detailed trading journal can transform your approach to Forex trading. By meticulously tracking every aspect of your trades—from the rationale and risk management to the emotional landscape—you build a comprehensive repository of knowledge. This habit allows you to refine your strategies, augment your strengths, and neutralize your weaknesses. Embrace the power of journaling as it empowers you to evolve into a disciplined, informed, and successful Forex trader.

Reviewing and Optimizing Your Approach

Reviewing and Optimizing Your Approach is crucial in achieving long-term success in Forex trading. This isn't just an occasional task but an ongoing process that ensures you continue to adapt and refine your strategies. Given the ever-changing nature of the Forex market, staying flexible and continuously learning from past trades can significantly enhance your trading performance.

First, let's acknowledge the importance of regularly reviewing your trading journal. This journal isn't just a record of your trades; it's a gold mine of information that, if analyzed properly, can yield insights into your trading habits, both good and bad. Regular reviews can help you identify patterns in your behavior and decisions that may need adjustment. Are you consistently entering trades too early? Are you letting emotions drive your exit strategy? Such questions can be answered by an honest and thorough review of your journal.

A practical approach to reviewing your trading journal can be breaking it down into weekly, monthly, and quarterly reviews. Weekly reviews offer a short-term perspective, allowing you to make quick adjustments if you notice any glaring issues. For instance, if you've noticed that you've had a particularly bad week due to over-leveraging or emotional trading, a quick corrective measure can be implemented promptly. Monthly and quarterly reviews, on the other hand, offer a more long-term perspective, allowing you to see trends and patterns that may not be apparent in shorter time frames.

Once you've gathered insights from your trading journal, the next step is optimization. One way to optimize your trading approach is through the process of backtesting. Backtesting involves applying your trading strategy to historical data to see how it would have performed. This gives you a valuable perspective on the effectiveness of your strategy without risking real money. Be honest and critical during backtesting. If a strategy doesn't yield the results you expected, don't hesitate to tweak or even completely overhaul it.

It's also worth noting that optimization isn't a one-time event either. Just as markets evolve, so too should your strategies. You should constantly seek to optimize your approaches based on both your personal experiences and prevailing market conditions. Sometimes, small tweaks can make a big difference in your overall performance. Perhaps adjusting your stop-loss levels or refining your entry criteria could significantly improve your results over time.

Another important aspect of reviewing and optimizing your approach involves staying current with market trends and news. The Forex market is influenced by a myriad of factors, including political events, economic indicators, and social changes. Having a keen understanding of these elements allows you to adapt your strategies to align with the current market environment. This is where continual learning and education come into play. Subscribing to financial news outlets, participating in webinars, and engaging in online trading communities can provide you with the information and insights needed to stay ahead of the curve.

Consider seeking feedback from more experienced traders, whether through forums, mentorship programs, or social trading platforms where you can observe and interact with other traders in real-time. Such interactions can offer invaluable perspectives and tips that you may not have considered. Sometimes, just a piece of advice or an alternative viewpoint can help you see an entirely different angle to your approach, providing room for improvement and optimization.

It's also imperative to evaluate the risk management strategies you've employed. When reviewing your trades, assess whether your risk management techniques were effective. Did you use stop losses and take profits appropriately? Were you too aggressive with leverage? By scrutinizing these aspects, you can make necessary adjustments to your risk management plan. The market can be unpredictable; hence a solid risk management strategy is essential to safeguard your capital.

Remember, your goal isn't just to make profitable trades but to ensure that your overall approach leads to sustained growth and minimal losses. Optimizing your approach often involves a balanced mix of being ambitious in your trading goals while being conservative in your risk management practices. Striking this balance can be nuanced, but it's achievable with constant review and refinement.

Emotions play a critical role in your trading performance. Review your emotional responses to your trades as part of your optimization process. If you experienced fear, greed, or impatience, identify which trades triggered these emotions and plan tactics to mitigate them in the future. This can include setting pre-defined rules for entering and exiting trades, practicing mindfulness techniques, or even taking breaks when you feel overwhelmed. Emotional discipline can significantly impact your trading outcomes, making it an essential focus in your review process.

Always keep an eye on technological advancements that could support your trading activities. Automated trading systems, algorithmic trading, and new analytical tools are continually emerging and could provide you with an edge. While human intuition and experience are irreplaceable, leveraging technology can augment your capabilities and streamline your trading process. Evaluating and integrating the right technological tools into your strategy should be part of your optimization routine.

Finally, make it a point to set actionable goals based on your reviews. Generic objectives like "become a better trader" are less effective than specific, measurable goals such as "reduce impulsive trades by 20% over the next quarter." By setting clear, achievable goals, you give yourself something tangible to work towards and measure your progress against. Use these goals as checkpoints to ensure that your approach is continuously evolving and improving.

In sum, **Reviewing and Optimizing Your Approach** is an ongoing cycle of assessment, adjustment, and advancement. With discipline, commitment, and a keen eye on both personal performance and market trends, you can create a robust, flexible trading strategy capable of navigating the complexities of the Forex market. Keep learning, keep evolving, and your efforts will undoubtedly result in more informed decisions and greater confidence in your trading journey.

CHAPTER 11:
STAYING INFORMED AND CONTINUAL LEARNING

As a new currency trader, staying informed and continually expanding your knowledge is crucial to your success. The Forex market is ever-changing, influenced by global events, economic shifts, and market sentiment. By following financial news diligently, exploring various online resources and forums, and engaging in continuous education through webinars and courses, you'll not only keep up with market movements but also sharpen your trading skills. Remember, the most successful traders are those who commit to lifelong learning, constantly refining their strategies and adapting to new information. Embrace the journey of perpetual improvement, as each piece of knowledge you gain becomes a building block towards more informed and confident trading decisions.

Following Financial News

Following Financial News is essential for anyone serious about mastering Forex trading. The currency market is heavily influenced by global economic events, political developments, and central bank policies. Staying updated with the latest financial news can help you make more informed trading decisions and anticipate market movements effectively. In this section, we'll explore the importance of following financial news and how it can give you an edge in your trading journey.

One of the primary reasons to stay on top of financial news is its direct impact on currency prices. Major economic indicators like GDP growth rates, unemployment figures, inflation data, and retail sales numbers can cause significant price fluctuations. For instance, a higher-than-expected GDP growth rate may lead to a stronger currency, while disappointing unemployment figures could weaken it. By keeping an eye on such reports, you can better predict how currency pairs might behave and adjust your trading strategies accordingly.

Political and geopolitical events are another critical factor that can sway the Forex market. Elections, government changes, trade agreements, and international conflicts can create uncertainty and volatility. Traders often react quickly to such news, causing sharp price movements. Understanding the political landscape and its potential impact on currencies can help you position yourself advantageously. For example, an unexpected election outcome might lead to a sudden depreciation of a currency, providing a valuable trading opportunity.

Central banks play a pivotal role in the currency market through their monetary policies. Changes in interest rates, quantitative easing programs, and other policy measures can have a profound effect on currency values. Regularly following announcements from central banks like the Federal Reserve, European Central Bank, Bank of Japan, and others can give you insights into their future actions. Predicting these policy shifts can help you anticipate market trends and make timely trades.

But how exactly do you keep up with all this information? There are several resources available that can help you stay informed. Financial news websites like Bloomberg, Reuters, and CNBC provide real-time updates on economic events and market-moving news. Subscribing to their newsletters or following them on social media can ensure you don't miss important updates. Additionally, economic calendars list upcoming releases of key economic indicators, helping you prepare for potential market shifts.

Moreover, understanding the content and implications of financial news requires some practice and a keen eye. It's not just about knowing what's happening but also interpreting how these events might influence the Forex market. For instance, if a central bank hints at tightening monetary policy due to rising inflation, it's a cue that the currency might strengthen. On the contrary, if geopolitical tensions escalate, it could lead to a flight to safe-haven currencies like the US dollar or the Swiss franc.

One strategy to leverage financial news is to combine it with your existing technical analysis skills. For example, if you notice a strong support level on a currency pair and there's an upcoming economic announcement likely to influence the currency positively, you might decide to enter a buy position. This combination of fundamental and technical analysis can provide a more comprehensive trading approach, enhancing your probability of success.

However, it's essential to exercise caution and not become overwhelmed by the sheer volume of information available. Developing a focused approach can help you filter out noise and concentrate on the news that truly matters. Start by identifying the key economic indicators, central bank announcements, and political events that are most relevant to the currencies you trade. Creating a routine for monitoring financial news can streamline the process and make it more manageable.

In addition, consider setting up alerts for specific news events related to your trading interests. Many financial news platforms allow you to customize notifications for particular economic releases or political developments. This way, you can stay informed without constantly monitoring the news, allowing you to concentrate on other aspects of your trading strategy.

Let's not forget the power of social media and online forums. Platforms like Twitter, LinkedIn, and specialized trading forums can be valuable sources of real-time information and insights. Following influential analysts, economists, and traders can provide you with diverse perspectives and help you gauge market sentiment. Just exercise discretion and verify information from multiple reliable sources to avoid falling for rumors or misinformation.

Adapting to the ever-evolving nature of financial news is a skill that can be honed over time. As you get more experienced, you'll become better at discerning which news stories are likely to have a significant impact and which are merely background noise. This discernment is critical to focus your mental and emotional energy on the most crucial information, leading to more effective and strategic trading decisions.

To make the most of your news-following efforts, it's also beneficial to keep a trading journal. Documenting how different news events have impacted your trades can provide valuable insights over time. Reviewing these journal entries can help you identify patterns and refine your strategies. You'll be able to see how accurately you predicted market movements based on news and where there might be room for improvement.

Finally, following financial news isn't just about reacting to events after they happen. It's also about learning to anticipate future developments and positioning yourself accordingly. Paying attention to trends and patterns in the news can help you forecast potential market movements. For example, consistent positive economic data from a country might indicate that its central bank will consider raising interest rates in the near future, leading to a stronger currency.

In conclusion, staying updated with financial news is a critical aspect of successful Forex trading. By understanding the impact of economic indicators, political events, and central bank policies, you can make more informed and strategic trading decisions. Utilize various news resources, develop a focused approach, and leverage both technical and fundamental analysis to stay ahead in the market. Over time, you'll sharpen your ability to anticipate market movements based on news events, ultimately enhancing your trading performance.

Online Resources and Forums

Online Resources and Forums play a critical role in the modern trader's education and continual growth. In today's interconnected digital world, the depth of information and the breadth of perspectives available online can vastly accelerate your learning curve. Forex trading isn't just about understanding charts and economic indicators; it's also about leveraging collective wisdom and staying informed about real-time market developments.

First, let's tackle online resources. Websites like Investopedia and BabyPips are veritable treasure troves of information. Whether you're looking to deepen your understanding of fundamental analysis or find tutorials on technical indicators, these platforms offer well-structured, beginner-friendly content. They break down complex topics into digestible chunks, allowing you to progress at your own pace. Furthermore, interactive features like quizzes and forums help reinforce your learning, making these resources indispensable for anyone serious about gaining Forex knowledge.

Various financial news websites like Bloomberg, Reuters, and CNBC provide up-to-the-minute news about the Forex market. Subscribing to newsletters or setting up news alerts can help you stay on top of breaking news that could impact your trades. These news outlets offer not just raw information, but nuanced analyses and expert opinions that can provide valuable context for making trading decisions. Being away from your trading desk doesn't mean you have to be disconnected from the market. Mobile apps from these news organizations can bring the news directly to your phone, ensuring you're always in the know.

Another invaluable resource is the array of downloadable eBooks and whitepapers available online. Many experienced traders and analysts have compiled their years of knowledge into comprehensive guides that are accessible for free or at minimal cost. Websites dedicated to Forex education often compile lists of recommended readings, categorizing them based on difficulty level and specific areas of interest. These reads can provide deeper insights that aren't covered in standard articles or blog posts. They offer the kind of wisdom and nuanced understanding gained only through years of experience in the market.

Online courses and webinars also deserve mention. Platforms like Coursera, Udemy, and even YouTube host countless courses on various aspects of Forex trading. These can range from short tutorial videos to comprehensive courses that span several hours. Webinars, in particular, are an excellent way to learn because they often feature interactive Q&A sessions, which allows participants to clarify doubts on the spot. Experts in the field often host these webinars, providing not just theoretical knowledge but also practical tips and real-world examples.

When it comes to direct interaction with other traders, forums are invaluable. Participating in forums such as Forex Factory, Trade2Win, and Elite Trader can provide you with diverse perspectives and encourage discussion about strategies, market conditions, and trading experiences. The sense of community in these forums is especially beneficial for beginners. You can find threads dedicated to almost every conceivable topic in Forex trading. From novice questions to advanced trading systems, there's something for everyone.

The value of forums isn't limited to the information you receive. Actively participating in these communities can also force you to articulate your thoughts and reasoning, thereby solidifying your own understanding. Answering questions, offering insights, and debating strategies can be a formative experience. The back-and-forth dialogue with other traders can expose you to new techniques and help you view the market from multiple angles. This collaborative learning process is a cornerstone of effective education in the realm of Forex trading.

Social media platforms like Twitter and LinkedIn also offer opportunities for learning and engagement. Following key figures in the Forex community, such as top analysts, experienced traders, and financial journalists, can provide you with regular insights and trading tips. Twitter, in particular, is a goldmine for real-time information and quick market updates. The use of hashtags can help you filter this information according to your interests. For instance, hashtags like #Forex, #TradingTips, and #FX can curate content specific to those subjects, making it easier for you to find relevant updates.

Many successful traders and Forex educators also maintain personal blogs where they share their trading experiences, strategies, and thoughts on market trends. Reading these blogs can offer unique, first-hand insights that aren't available in traditional educational resources. Personal stories of losses and gains can be particularly instructive, offering lessons that purely theoretical content can't provide. Often, these blogs include charts, statistics, and screenshots that make the learning process much more interactive and visually engaging.

It's also worth mentioning the importance of subscription-based services which offer premium content and advanced tools for serious traders. Websites like TradingView offer detailed charting tools and market analysis, often paired with community features where traders can publish and discuss their trading ideas. Subscription services can provide more refined tools and analytics, which are particularly useful for advanced traders who need more than just basic information to inform their trading decisions.

To efficiently keep track of the information you gather from these various sources, consider using tools like Evernote or OneNote. These note-taking applications allow you to organize your research, create summaries, and jot down ideas for future trades. By maintaining a well-organized repository of your learning materials, you can easily revisit important concepts and strategies at any time. This practice not only reinforces your knowledge but also helps in the continuous refinement of your trading strategies.

Don't underestimate the power of local and global trading communities. Meetups and online communities can provide face-to-face interaction, which can add another layer of depth to your learning. Websites like Meetup.com often list local Forex trading groups where individuals gather to share knowledge and experiences. These interactions can provide real-time feedback and foster mentorship opportunities that can be immensely beneficial for novice traders.

Participating in online competitions and trading challenges can also be both educational and rewarding. Many brokers and trading platforms host these events, providing an opportunity to hone your skills in a competitive environment. These challenges often come with valuable prizes, ranging from cash rewards to advanced trading software. More importantly, they offer practical, hands-on experience, which is crucial for mastering the art of Forex trading.

In conclusion, the array of online resources and forums available to modern traders is staggering. By leveraging these tools effectively, you can significantly accelerate your learning curve and gain a deeper, more nuanced understanding of the Forex market. The key is to remain engaged, continually seek out new information, and participate actively in the trading community. With the right balance of study and practice, you'll be well on your way to becoming a confident and knowledgeable Forex trader.

Continuous Education and Webinars

Continuous Education and Webinars are pivotal when it comes to maintaining your edge in the ever-changing landscape of Forex trading. The Forex market is renowned for its dynamism, influenced by an array of economic, political, and social factors that can shift trends in the blink of an eye. Becoming adept at navigating these waters requires a commitment to perpetual learning and adaptability. Thankfully, the wealth of resources available—in particular, webinars—help traders stay sharp and informed.

Continuous education is fundamental for anyone serious about Forex trading. It's not just about acquiring knowledge, but about staying current with the latest market trends, technological advancements, and regulatory changes. Forex markets don't stand still, and neither should you. Successful traders understand this and invest in their education as a way to maintain their competitive edge and refine their trading strategies. This constant learning cycle ensures they're prepared for whatever the market throws their way.

Webinars represent one of the most accessible and effective methods for ongoing education. These online seminars are typically hosted by industry experts who bring a wealth of experience and insights to the table. By participating in webinars, you can gain direct access to valuable information and actionable strategies, all from the comfort of your own home. They're often interactive, allowing you to ask questions and engage in discussions with the host and other participants.

One of the benefits of webinars is their ability to cover a wide range of topics. Whether you're looking to understand the nuances of technical analysis, get insights into fundamental economic indicators, or learn about the psychological aspects of trading, there's likely a webinar out there for you. These sessions can range from beginner to advanced levels, making them suitable for traders at any stage of their journey. They also often delve into timely topics that reflect current market conditions, ensuring the information is relevant and up-to-date.

The flexibility that webinars offer can't be overstated. Many of them are recorded and made available online, giving you the ability to watch them at your convenience. This on-demand feature is particularly beneficial for those who may have other commitments or reside in different time zones. With the ability to pause, rewind, and re-watch parts of the webinar, you can ensure you thoroughly understand and absorb the information being presented.

Quality webinars often include practical demonstrations and real-time analyses. These elements bring theoretical knowledge to life, transforming abstract concepts into concrete examples. When experts demonstrate their strategies on live charts or perform real-time analyses, they provide an invaluable hands-on learning experience. This can help bridge the gap between theory and practice, making it easier to apply what you've learned when you're trading on your own.

However, not all webinars are created equal. It's essential to be discerning when choosing which ones to attend. Look for webinars hosted by reputable trading organizations or well-known industry experts. Check for reviews or testimonials from other participants to gauge the quality of the content. Webinars that offer courses with comprehensive curriculums and provide additional resources are often more valuable.

Interaction with guest speakers during webinars can also offer a wealth of knowledge. These experts often share their personal experiences, including both their successes and failures. This candidness can provide insightful lessons that go beyond what you might find in textbooks or standard online articles. Engaging with experts can also help you stay motivated and inspired, seeing firsthand what's possible with dedication and continuous learning.

Another significant advantage of webinars is the opportunity for networking. Many webinars include forums or chat features that allow participants to connect with each other. Networking with other traders can provide new perspectives and insights that you might not have considered on your own. It can also be a source of support and encouragement, especially if you're navigating challenges in your trading journey.

In addition to webinars, many trading platforms and brokerage firms offer continuous education programs. These programs may include video tutorials, e-books, articles, and other learning materials. The comprehensive nature of these programs means you can learn at your own pace, focusing on the areas where you need the most improvement. Taking advantage of these resources ensures you're continually enhancing your skills and staying informed about the latest in Forex trading.

Remember, the goal is not just to accumulate knowledge but to apply it effectively. Continuous education should translate into improved trading performance and better decision-making abilities. By actively participating in webinars and seeking out educational resources, you're not just expanding your knowledge base but also refining your skills and strategies. This proactive approach to education can set you apart in the competitive world of Forex trading.

As you progress in your trading journey, you'll find that the landscape evolves, and new challenges emerge. Continuous education ensures you're not just reacting to changes but anticipating them and adjusting your strategies accordingly. By remaining a lifelong learner, you're setting yourself up for sustained success in the Forex market.

CHAPTER 12:
COMMON PITFALLS AND HOW TO AVOID THEM

In your journey through the Forex market, it's critical to be aware of common mistakes that can sabotage your trading success. Overtrading and undertrading are two sides of the same coin, often stemming from either overconfidence or hesitancy. Both can deplete your capital if not managed correctly. Adapting to market changes is equally important, as sticking rigidly to a strategy without considering new data can lead to missed opportunities or bigger losses. Neglecting risk management is arguably the most dangerous pitfall; always set stop-losses to guard against unexpected market movements and never risk more than you're willing to lose. By staying vigilant about these common errors, you can hone your skills and make wiser, more calculated decisions in your trading activities.

Overtrading and Undertrading

Overtrading and Undertrading are two common pitfalls that new traders often encounter, impacting their potential for success in the Forex market. Understanding these issues and knowing how to navigate them can help you maintain a balanced approach to trading and increase your chances of long-term profitability.

Overtrading occurs when a trader executes trades too frequently or takes on too many positions at once. This behavior is usually driven by emotions such as greed, fear of missing out (FOMO), or a desire to recover previous losses quickly. Overtrading can lead to high transaction costs, poor decision-making, and ultimately, substantial financial losses. It's a trap that can be easy to fall into, especially for enthusiastic beginners who are keen to see rapid results.

Imagine you've just experienced a winning trade. The excitement and adrenaline might push you to enter another trade immediately, assuming the market trend will continue. However, this emotional decision can blind you to the necessary analysis and due diligence required before placing a new trade. The market doesn't move based solely on your previous successes; it's an independent entity that requires constant, unbiased analysis.

On the flip side, undertrading is just as detrimental. Undertrading happens when a trader executes too few trades, often driven by fear of making mistakes or a lack of confidence in their analysis. This cautious approach can prevent you from leveraging good trading opportunities, thus hindering your ability to build experience and improve your trading skills. While it's essential to avoid jumping on every market opportunity, paralysis by analysis can stifle your growth and limit your learning.

A balanced approach in Forex trading involves finding the sweet spot between overtrading and undertrading. This balance is not just about the number of trades you execute but also about the quality and rationale behind each trade. Focus on developing a sound trading strategy and sticking to it. Discipline is key. Your strategy should include clear guidelines on when to enter and exit trades, how much capital to risk, and the overall market conditions favorable for your trading style.

Let's delve a bit deeper into the risks and consequences of overtrading. When you frequently enter and exit positions, transaction costs can accumulate, eroding your profits. Every trade involves a spread or commission, meaning that even if you make a series of small profits, the fees can diminish your net gains. Not to mention, overtrading often results in stress and emotional burnout. The constant monitoring and reacting can take a toll on your mental and emotional well-being.

Overtrading is also symptomatic of a lack of a solid trading plan. Traders who lack a well-defined strategy often end up making impulsive decisions, driven by emotions rather than logic and analysis. This can result in entering trades that don't align with your risk tolerance, trading plan, or market analysis – a recipe for disaster in the long run.

To avoid overtrading, you need to develop a comprehensive trading plan and adhere to it diligently. Your plan should include criteria for trade entries and exits, risk management rules, and guidelines for analyzing market conditions. Stick to your plan, and resist the urge to deviate from it, even if a seemingly irresistible trading opportunity presents itself. Consistency and discipline are your best allies in the chaotic world of Forex markets.

Now, let's talk about undertrading. While exercising caution in trading is essential, being overly cautious can hinder your progress. Undertrading often stems from fear – fear of losing money, fear of making mistakes, or fear of the unknown. It's characterized by missing out on potential trading opportunities, not entering trades even when signals align with your strategy, and perpetually waiting for the "perfect" market conditions that may never come.

To overcome undertrading, start by building confidence in your trading strategy. Practice is key. Use demo accounts to test your strategies without the pressure of real money. Track your trades, analyze outcomes, and learn from your mistakes. As you gain confidence, gradually transition to live trading with small positions, increasing your trade frequency as you become more comfortable.

Another effective way to counter undertrading is to set clear, attainable goals for your trading activities. This could include a target number of trades per week or month. Having specific goals helps you stay focused and committed to executing trades, reducing the tendency to hold back due to fear or uncertainty.

Educational resources and continual learning play a significant role in finding the right balance between overtrading and undertrading. Keep yourself informed about market trends, emerging strategies, and lessons from other successful traders. Participate in trading forums, attend webinars, and read books to broaden your understanding and improve your trading skills.

The emotional aspect of trading can't be ignored when discussing overtrading and undertrading. Developing emotional discipline is crucial. Overtrading often results from an inability to manage the excitement of winning trades, while undertrading is usually a result of succumbing to fear. Psychological resilience and emotional control will help you maintain a calm and rational approach to trading.

Remember, Forex trading is a journey. Balancing between overtrading and undertrading requires patience, practice, and continuous improvement. As you progress, you'll find that maintaining this balance is not only about sticking to a strategy but also about understanding yourself, recognizing your emotional triggers, and adapting accordingly.

In conclusion, the key to avoiding overtrading and undertrading lies in self-awareness, discipline, and a well-crafted trading plan. By focusing on quality over quantity, continuously educating yourself, and developing emotional control, you can navigate these common pitfalls and increase your chances of long-term success in the Forex market. Your trading journey will be filled with ups and downs, but finding the right balance will empower you to make informed and confident trading decisions.

Failing to Adapt to Market Changes

Failing to Adapt to Market Changes can be a detrimental mistake for any trader, especially for those new to Forex trading. Market conditions in the Forex world are not static; they are influenced by a myriad of factors, including economic shifts, political events, and even natural disasters. Therefore, an inflexible trading strategy can quickly become outdated and lead to significant losses.

One of the first steps to avoiding this pitfall is to understand that the Forex market is dynamic. Currency values fluctuate based on real-time events and data releases. Traders who don't stay updated with these changes risk making decisions based on outdated information. This can lead to missed opportunities or, even worse, taking positions that are no longer viable.

Consider the importance of staying abreast with economic indicators. Reports like GDP, employment numbers, and inflation rates can dramatically affect currency prices. If your trading strategy doesn't take these indicators into account or fails to allow for flexibility in the face of new data, you could find yourself on the losing side of a trade.

Moreover, political and geopolitical events are critical in shaping market conditions. Trade wars, elections, and international agreements can cause significant volatility. Ignoring these factors or assuming that your trading strategy can weather any political storm is a recipe for failure.

Adaptability doesn't just mean reacting to news; it also means having a proactive stance in adjusting your strategies. For example, during periods of low volatility, a range-bound strategy might be effective. However, if volatility suddenly spikes, continuing to use the same strategy without adjustment could be disastrous. Being able to shift strategies based on market conditions, such as shifting from a range-bound approach to a breakout strategy during periods of high volatility, is key.

A flexible trading strategy often includes diversifying your tools and methods. Relying on a single technical indicator or strategy may work in some conditions but fail in others. Experienced traders continually evaluate the effectiveness of their tools and are willing to incorporate new ones. This might mean learning to use different technical indicators, adopting new trading platforms, or even learning new trading methods altogether.

Backtesting is another critical component in adapting to market changes. Regularly backtest your strategies against historical data and recent market conditions. This practice can reveal weaknesses in your current approach and highlight areas for improvement. It's a way to validate whether your strategy holds up over time and under various market conditions.

Additionally, maintaining a trading journal offers invaluable insights. By keeping a detailed record of your trades, including entry and exit points, the rationale behind each trade, and the results, you can identify patterns in your own behavior and in the market. Reviewing your journal allows you to see what has worked and what hasn't, making it easier to adjust your strategies accordingly.

The psychology of trading also plays a significant role in adapting to market changes. Emotional discipline is essential when facing a shift in market conditions. Fear and greed can drive poor decision-making, particularly when the market moves in unexpected directions. Successful traders maintain composure, sticking to their revised strategies rather than reacting emotionally to market swings.

Another critical aspect is risk management. While this will be covered in more detail in other sections, it's worth mentioning here that proper risk management strategies can help protect against unforeseen market shifts. Using tools like stop-loss orders and adjusting leverage can prevent catastrophic losses when the market doesn't behave as expected.

Education and continual learning also bolster your ability to adapt. The Forex market continually evolves, and staying informed through financial news, online resources, forums, and webinars can keep your strategies up-to-date. Continuous education allows you to spot emerging trends and adapt your strategies before most others do.

Lastly, it's important to cultivate a mindset of growth and learning. Forex trading isn't just about making quick profits but understanding that the market is a complex system influenced by numerous factors. An adaptable trader sees each market shift not as a threat, but as an opportunity to learn and refine their strategy.

In conclusion, failing to adapt to market changes can greatly hinder your success in Forex trading. By staying informed, regularly backtesting and adjusting your strategies, maintaining a trading journal, and managing risk effectively, you position yourself to navigate the ever-changing market conditions. Remember, adaptability isn't just a skill; it's a mindset that separates successful traders from the rest.

Neglecting Risk Management

Neglecting Risk Management is a critical misstep that many novice traders make, often leading to devastating consequences. Risk management is the backbone of any successful trading strategy. Being new to Forex trading, you might feel tempted to dive headfirst into trades without considering the potential downside. The lure of quick profits can be overwhelming, but disregarding risk management can quickly turn those dreams into nightmares.

Imagine you've identified what appears to be a perfect trade: a currency pair that's trending favorably, supported by solid technical indicators. You're confident and excited, so you decide to invest a significant portion of your capital. However, no one can predict the market with 100% accuracy. Without proper risk management, if the market moves against you, your loss will be substantial, possibly wiping out a significant portion of your trading account.

Let's break it down: One of the most crucial aspects of risk management is setting stop loss and take profit levels. This is essentially your safety net, your insurance policy against unexpected market movements. By defining these parameters, you're setting a limit on how much you're willing to lose and a target for your gains. Failure to set these levels is akin to sailing a ship without life jackets onboard. It's not about having a pessimistic outlook; it's about being prepared for all possible scenarios.

Beyond stop loss and take profit, managing leverage and margin is another vital element. Forex trading offers high leverage, which can amplify gains but also magnify losses. Misunderstanding or misusing leverage can lead to margin calls where you're forced to deposit more funds or close positions at a loss. It's essential to use leverage wisely and understand the risks associated with it. Always remember, leverage is a double-edged sword.

Then, there's the 1% risk rule—a fundamental guideline in risk management. This rule suggests that you should never risk more than 1% of your capital on a single trade. It may seem overly cautious, but this conservative approach is key to long-term survival in the Forex market. Neglecting this rule can lead to significant losses, putting immense pressure on your remaining capital to recover, a task that becomes increasingly difficult as losses mount.

Neglecting risk management can also trap you in a cycle of emotional trading. When you experience a significant loss, the instinctive reaction is to try to make that money back quickly. This leads to revenge trading—making hasty, emotional trades to recover losses, often resulting in even greater financial damage. Maintaining emotional discipline is imperative, but it's nearly impossible without a solid risk management strategy.

Another subtle yet dangerous risk is underestimating market volatility. Economic indicators, political events, and geopolitical upheavals can create sudden, drastic shifts in currency values. Without a risk management plan, you're exposed to the full brunt of these swings, which can dramatically affect your positions. By being prepared for volatility, through methods such as diversifying your trades and using proper position sizing, you can better withstand these market tremors.

Finally, consistent application of risk management techniques defines the difference between gambling and trading. While gambling relies on luck, trading—especially in the Forex market—should be a calculated endeavor. Successful traders aren't always the ones making the biggest profits; they're the ones consistently applying their risk management strategies to protect their capital and live to trade another day.

In summary, neglecting risk management is like building a house on a shaky foundation. While the structure may hold for a while, any significant stress will bring it crashing down. In the volatile world of Forex trading, having a rigorous risk management plan is non-negotiable. It's not an insurance against losing trades, but rather a system to ensure that no single loss has the power to derail your trading journey permanently. Equip yourself with risk management techniques, and you will navigate the Forex market with greater confidence and resilience.

Online Review Request for This Book

If you found this book helpful in navigating the complexities of Forex trading and steering clear of common pitfalls, please consider leaving an online review to help others embark on their trading journey with confidence.

Turning Pips into Profit - Your Journey Forward

Congratulations! You've embarked on the fascinating journey of Forex trading, gaining a wealth of knowledge that positions you ahead of many aspiring traders. While you've learned about the foundational elements, it's important to remember that the real voyage begins now. The concepts, strategies, and tools we've discussed are the building blocks for your future success.

It's not just about accumulating knowledge; it's about implementation and continuous learning. Forex markets evolve, and so should your strategies and understanding. Start with small trades, keep your emotions in check, and fine-tune your approach as you go. Patience is not just a virtue in trading; it's a necessity. Taking the time to reflect on each trade will pay dividends.

Remember: Every pip potential comes with risk. Managing that risk will determine whether you turn those pips into sustained profits. Implementing the risk management techniques highlighted, such as setting stop-loss orders and adhering to the 1% risk rule, will safeguard your capital and create a safety net for your trading activities.

You've also been equipped with the psychological tools necessary to navigate the tumultuous emotional landscape of trading. Mastering emotional discipline, overcoming fear and greed, and cultivating patience will be your allies in making objective, rational decisions even in volatile market conditions.

Continue to hone your technical and fundamental analysis skills. These analytical tools will allow you to read market trends and make educated guesses on currency movements. Through the consistent application and continual scepticism of your analysis, you will improve your accuracy over time.

Forex trading is a dynamic field, and adaptability is crucial. Markets shift, economic policies change, and unexpected geopolitical events can send ripples through currencies globally. Stay informed by following financial news and subscribing to relevant forums and webinars. Always be on the lookout for new techniques and strategies that can enhance your trading arsenal.

Keeping a trading journal isn't just a recommended practice—it's indispensable. Documenting each trade, annotating the rationale behind each decision, and reflecting on the outcomes will provide invaluable insights into your trading patterns and behaviors. This constant review process will help you identify areas of strength and those needing improvement, fostering a cycle of continuous refinement and growth.

Avoid common pitfalls such as overtrading and undertrading. Both extremes can harm your account balance and emotional stability. Maintain consistency in your approach and stick to your trading plan, but also remain flexible enough to adjust when market conditions necessitate it. Always prioritize risk management to sustain your journey.

The road ahead is as exciting as it is challenging. The tools and knowledge you've gained are the rungs of the ladder that will lead you to success. There is no end to growth and learning in Forex trading, and each day brings an opportunity to improve on the last.

Turning pips into profit requires dedication, discipline, and a relentless pursuit of knowledge. You've got the foundation; now it's up to you to build upon it. Engage with fellow traders, seek mentorship, and never stop learning. The journey might be long, but with perseverance and a keen eye on the market, the rewards can be substantial.

So, go forth with confidence. The Forex market is vast with countless opportunities waiting. Embrace the challenges, learn from the setbacks, and celebrate the victories. Your journey forward is filled with limitless potential, and the profits are just the beginning. Here's to turning those pips into the profit you aspire for!

Forex Glossary

The world of Forex trading comes with its own set of terminology. Understanding these terms is essential for navigating the market effectively. Here, we introduce some of the key terms you'll encounter as you start your journey in Forex trading.

Ask Price

The ask price, also known as the offer price, is the lowest price a seller is willing to accept for a currency. When you buy a currency pair, you'll be quoted the ask price.

Bid Price

The bid price is the highest price a buyer is willing to pay for a currency. When you sell a currency pair, you'll be quoted the bid price.

Currency Pair

A currency pair consists of two currencies, with one being quoted against the other. The first currency in the pair is the base currency, and the second is the quote currency. For example, in the EUR/USD pair, EUR is the base currency, and USD is the quote currency.

Leverage

Leverage allows traders to control a large position with a small amount of capital. It's expressed as a ratio, such as 50:1, meaning you can trade $50 for every $1 in your account. While leverage can amplify gains, it can also magnify losses.

Margin

Margin is the amount of money required to open a leveraged trading position. It represents a fraction of the total trade size. Properly managing margin is crucial to avoid margin calls and potential losses.

Pip

A pip, or percentage in point, is the smallest price movement in a currency pair's exchange rate. For most pairs, a pip represents the fourth decimal place (0.0001), except for pairs involving the Japanese yen, where it's the second decimal place (0.01).

Spread

The spread is the difference between the bid price and the ask price of a currency pair. It represents the cost of trading, and a narrower spread typically indicates a more liquid market.

Lot

A lot is a standard unit of measurement in Forex trading. There are three types of lots: standard (100,000 units), mini (10,000 units), and micro (1,000 units). Different lot sizes allow traders to manage their risk more precisely.

Stop-Loss Order

A stop-loss order is an order placed with a broker to buy or sell once the price reaches a certain level. It's used to limit potential losses on a trade by closing the position at a pre-determined price.

Take-Profit Order

A take-profit order is an order to close a position when the price reaches a certain profit level. It helps lock in profits by automatically closing the trade at your desired price target.

Swap

Swap, or rollover interest, is the interest paid or earned for holding a position overnight. It's determined by the interest rate differential between the two currencies in the pair. A positive swap earns interest, while a negative swap incurs a cost.

Volatility

Volatility refers to the degree of variation in the price of a currency pair over time. Higher volatility means greater price swings, which can present both opportunities and risks for traders.

Understanding these fundamental terms will serve as a solid foundation for your Forex trading journey. Keep this glossary handy as a reference as you navigate the exciting world of currency trading.

APPENDIX A:
SAMPLE TRADING PLAN

Creating a robust trading plan is like building a house; it needs a solid foundation. This sample trading plan highlights the key elements that every new Forex trader should consider. Remember, while this plan is a great starting point, it's essential to tailor it to fit your unique goals, risk tolerance, and trading style.

1. Trading Goals

- **Short-Term Goals:** Specify what you aim to achieve on a daily or weekly basis. This might include gaining a certain number of pips per week or honing a specific trading strategy.

- **Long-Term Goals:** Define what you'd like to achieve within a year or beyond. This could involve reaching a specific return on investment (ROI) or achieving a professional trading certification.

2. Risk Management

- **Risk Per Trade:** Decide on the amount or percentage of your trading capital you're willing to risk per trade. Most experts recommend not exceeding 1-2% per trade.

- **Stop Loss and Take Profit:** Establish criteria for setting stop loss and take profit orders. Staying consistent here is crucial to managing risk effectively.

- **Risk-Reward Ratio:** Determine your minimum risk-reward ratio. A common ratio is 1:3, meaning you're willing to risk $1 to make $3.

3. Trading Strategy

- **Type of Strategy:** Choose a primary trading strategy such as scalping, day trading, swing trading, or position trading. Make sure this aligns with your schedule and personality.

- **Technical Indicators:** List the technical indicators you'll rely on. This might include moving averages, RSI, and MACD among others.

- **Fundamental Analysis:** Decide how you'll incorporate fundamental analysis into your trading. This could involve monitoring economic indicators, news events, or central bank pronouncements.

4. Market Analysis

- **Currency Pairs:** Choose the currency pairs you'll focus on. Many beginners start with major pairs like EUR/USD, GBP/USD, and USD/JPY.

- **Timeframes:** Select the timeframe you'll use for analysis and trades. Common options range from 1-minute charts to daily charts.

5. Trading Routine

- **Pre-Market Preparation:** Outline your routine before the market opens. This might involve reviewing key economic events for the day and analyzing overnight market movements.

- **During Market Hours:** Describe what you'll do while the market is open, from monitoring trades to adjusting stop loss levels.

- **Post-Market Review:** Establish a routine for reviewing your trades after the market closes. Analyze what went well and identify areas for improvement.

6. Record Keeping

- **Trading Journal:** Maintain a detailed trading journal where you log every trade, including entry and exit points, the rationale behind the trade, and the outcome.

- **Monthly Review:** Conduct a comprehensive review of your trading activity at the end of each month. Assess your performance against your goals and make adjustments as needed.

This sample trading plan serves as a template to build upon. Remember, the most successful traders are those who continually refine their plans based on experience and market changes. Keep learning, stay disciplined, and most importantly, don't be afraid to adapt.

With your trading plan in hand, you're not just entering the Forex market—you're prepared to navigate it with purpose and precision. May your journey be both profitable and enlightening.

APPENDIX B:
RECOMMENDED READING
AND RESOURCES

Diving into the world of Forex trading can be both exciting and a bit overwhelming. Knowledge is indeed power, and equipping yourself with the right resources can make a huge difference in your trading journey. Below, we've compiled a list of highly recommended books and resources that will give you deeper insights into various aspects of Forex trading. This collection is tailored to help you build a solid foundation and inspire confidence in your trading decisions.

Essential Books on Forex Trading

- **"Currency Trading for Dummies" by Brian Dolan**

This book is perfect for beginners. It breaks down complex concepts into easily digestible bits, helping newbies understand the foundational aspects of Forex trading.

- **"Day Trading and Swing Trading the Currency Market" by Kathy Lien**

Kathy Lien provides insight into both day and swing trading strategies, offering practical advice and detailed explanations on technical and fundamental analyses.

- **"The Little Book of Currency Trading" by Kathy Lien**

Another gem by Kathy Lien, this book simplifies currency trading strategies and makes the content accessible for readers at all levels.

- **"Japanese Candlestick Charting Techniques" by Steve Nison**

This book is a go-to for understanding how to use candlestick charts effectively, which is a critical skill for technical analysis in Forex.

- **"Trading in the Zone" by Mark Douglas**

Mark Douglas dives into the psychological aspects of trading, emphasizing the importance of mindset, discipline, and emotional control.

Helpful Websites and Online Forums

- **BabyPips (babypips.com)**

BabyPips offers a wealth of information for beginner traders, including educational articles, courses, and an active community forum.

- **Investopedia (investopedia.com)**

A great resource for financial education, Investopedia provides detailed articles on Forex trading concepts and a comprehensive Forex dictionary.

- **TradingView (tradingview.com)**

This platform offers advanced charting tools, a vibrant community of traders, and the ability to share and discuss trading ideas.

- **Forex Factory (forexfactory.com)**

Forex Factory is well-known for its economic calendar, forums, and market analysis tools, making it a valuable resource for staying informed.

- **Myfxbook (myfxbook.com)**

Myfxbook offers an array of tools for traders, including portfolio tracking, social trading, and performance analytics.

Continued Education and Webinars

- **FXStreet (fxstreet.com)**

FXStreet offers regular webinars on various trading topics, presented by experienced traders and analysts.

- **Forex.com (forex.com)**

The Forex.com Educational Center provides webinars, tutorials, and articles to help you deepen your trading knowledge.

- **DailyFX (dailyfx.com)**

DailyFX offers educational webcasts, articles, and in-depth market analysis to keep you informed about market trends and strategies.

Trading in the Forex market is a continuous journey of learning and adapting. These resources will not only provide you with foundational knowledge but also keep you updated with the latest trends and strategies. Remember, the more you learn, the better equipped you'll be to navigate the dynamic world of Forex trading with confidence.

Printed in Great Britain
by Amazon